THE MIDDLE SCHOOL STUDENT'S GUIDE TO ACADEMIC

THE MIDDLE SCHOOL STUDENT'S GUIDE TO ACADEMIC

Success:

12 CONVERSATIONS

FOR COLLEGE AND CAREER READINESS

BY **BLAKE NEMELKA**
AND
BO NEMELKA

Portions previously published as *Beat the Middle*

With a foreword by
Sean Covey, bestselling author of
The 7 Habits of Highly Effective Teens

Simon & Schuster Books for Young Readers
New York   London   Toronto   Sydney   New Delhi

SIMON & SCHUSTER BOOKS FOR YOUNG READERS
An imprint of Simon & Schuster Children's Publishing Division
1230 Avenue of the Americas, New York, New York 10020
Copyright © 2014, 2016 by Franklin Covey Co.
An earlier edition of this book was published in 2014 as *Beat the Middle:*
The Middle School Student's Guide to Academic Success.
Names of some of the people portrayed have been changed.
SIMON & SCHUSTER BOOKS FOR YOUNG READERS is a trademark of
Simon & Schuster, Inc.
Franklin Covey Co. and the Franklin Covey Co. logo are trademarks of Franklin
Covey Co. and their use is by permission.
For information about special discounts for bulk purchases, please contact Simon &
Schuster Special Sales at 1-866-506-1949 or business@simonandschuster.com.
The Simon & Schuster Speakers Bureau can bring authors to your live event. For
more information or to book an event, contact the Simon & Schuster Speakers
Bureau at 1-866-248-3049 or visit our website at www.simonspeakers.com.
Interior design by Candace Andersen
The text for this book was set in Century Gothic.
Manufactured in China
0616 SCP
First Simon & Schuster Books for Young Readers paperback edition August 2016
10 9 8 7 6 5 4 3 2 1
Library of Congress Cataloging-in-Publication Data
Names: Nemelka, Blake, author. | Nemelka, Bo, author.
Title: The middle school student's guide to academic success : 12 conversations for
college and career readiness / Blake Nemelka and Bo Nemelka.
Description: First Simon & Schuster Books for Young Readers paperback edition. |
New York : Simon & Schuster Books for Young Readers, 2016.
Identifiers: LCCN 2015038719 | ISBN 9781481471602 (paperback) |
ISBN 9781481471619 (ebook)
Subjects: LCSH: Middle school students—Life skills guides—Juvenile literature. |
Academic achievement—Juvenile literature. | Success—Juvenile literature. |
BISAC: JUVENILE NONFICTION / Study Aids / General. | JUVENILE NONFICTION /
School & Education. | JUVENILE NONFICTION / Activity Books.
Classification: LCC LB1135 .N46 2016 | DDC 373.236—dc23
LC record available at http://lccn.loc.gov/2015038719

CONTENTS

FOREWORD

SUCCESS. It's a word that you probably hear all the time.

Teachers, parents, and coaches are all likely driving home the importance of things you're doing now at school and in life for your future "success." And I bet I know what's crossed your mind a few times during these pep talks: "So what? My grades don't matter now. They'll count in high school." Or "Who cares about those silly clubs?" Or "What does what I do now matter for my future 'success'? I'm in middle school, for crying out loud."

Believe me, I get it. Today's world is full of a lot more pressures and they seem to be hitting us younger and younger. "Can't I just be a *kid*?" you might be thinking.

And you're right! You are still young and have plenty of time to figure out what you're going to do with the rest of your life. But your parents and teachers and coaches have been where you are and they may have a valid point.

Go with me for a second here. Say someday you want to be a doctor. Before you attain that goal, there are many other little successes you'll need to achieve first, such as getting into med school, going to college, and even just getting an A in high school biology.

But—now here's the cool part—each of these successes is built upon *even tinier* successes, and they're things that you *are* probably starting to do right now. Things like building good study habits so you can achieve that A in biology, or even just picking up this book.

When you take the first steps toward the little successes, you start getting into the habit of success, and once you get into the habit, those bigger steps won't seem so big, or scary. In fact, they'll be exciting, because you'll be totally ready for them.

In short, it's really *never* too early to start building these habits and thinking about your college and career future. You just have to get started. You have to begin with the end in mind.

This book will help you do that. *And* it'll make it fun.

Because Blake and Bo Nemelka (yep, twin brothers) understand what it's like to be in middle school. Really, they *get it*. They had worries and challenges very similar to the ones you have. But they also understood that overcoming them not just once, but all the time, would make them not just successful middle schoolers, but successful people in the long run. And it worked! Blake earned a master's degree in education administration from Vanderbilt University, and Bo received a master's in health-care management from Yale. And because they understand middle schoolers, they know you don't want to just be given a bunch of boring checklists of things to do. They're going to get you involved, invested, and excited about every step on this journey. They offer real-world examples of kids just like you and exercises to help you apply each aspect of their method to your goals and interests, your definition of *success*.

That's why this book is called *The Middle School Student's Guide to Academic Success: 12 Conversations for College and Career Readiness*. Each of the twelve topics is meant to be a dialogue, a conversation between you and the authors and between you and a parent or mentor who can help you take what you learn and apply it to your life. But remember, a conversation is a two-way street, and the advice and guidance offered here only works if you actively engage with it. Does that sound like work? Sure, but it's the enjoyable kind of work. Think of these conversations as your starting point, the foundation for all the exciting things ahead of you, and you get to start envisioning those exciting things right now!

So let's get started, get talking, get motivated. It's your future and *you* can make it a successful one—yes, even starting in middle school.

Sean Covey

A THOUGHT
TO PONDER

———— • ❦ • ————

"If you can dream it, you can do it."

—WALT DISNEY
AMERICAN ENTREPRENEUR, CARTOONIST, ANIMATOR, VOICE
ACTOR, AND FILM PRODUCER

A Note to
STUDENTS

IF YOU ARE A STUDENT READING THIS BOOK, you are awesome! You have taken the first, and perhaps most important, step to academic success. Just by starting this book you are showing that you are looking for a way to achieve success at school and in your life.

We want to help you.

It's rare for anyone to like their middle school years. It's a hard time. You have to get accustomed to a much larger school. Friends begin acting weird. Lockers never cooperate and open when you need them to. English teachers overwhelm you. Math teachers lose you. And those are just the things that are happening outside of you. We know that you may also be overwhelmed by what is happening inside of you and to you. It is a rough few years.

We understand that. We remember.

You do not know us. But because we are "adults" and have written this book, you might assume that we are ancient. We're not. Trust us. We remember middle school. Most importantly, we remember the steps we took and that our friends took to achieve success. That's what this book is all about.

This book, this guide, is for you. But this is not something you should have to read alone. You will need help from someone to begin applying parts of it, especially since there are sections that require someone to hold you accountable to the action items we will invite you to complete.

Please ask someone you trust to read this book with you and help you along the way, especially with the action items. We refer to these individuals throughout this book as parents/mentors. They are all around you—in your family, school, and community. Pick someone and start the journey together!

Let's start there—with the action items. We understand that action items sound suspiciously like homework. And it might even look a little bit like homework.

But it's *awesome* work.

It's *life-changing* work.

The key word here is work. Success takes work. And we want you to take it seriously—we want you to dig in and find out where you are now and make goals and plans for the future.

We hope the action items will challenge you, but we do not want you to ever be discouraged or give up. You can do this!

The action items are found at the end of every chapter or "Conversation." In this book we will have 12 Conversations. We refer to each chapter as a Conversation because we want you to be engaged in a dialogue—or conversation— with your parents/mentors. To help you put into practice what you have learned, we've included worksheets at the end of the Conversations. They are also available for download at http://www.theleaderinme.org/middleschoolsuccess.

We'll tell you what helped us and our friends, and you decide what you can do to improve and grow. It's not one-sided.

If we just talked and shared and you put the book down and walked away, it would be a failure. We want you to be completely engaged.

We chose the Conversation topics very carefully with the help of students, parents, mentors, and academic professionals. We believe these 12 things will help you now, tomorrow, and well into your future. These conversations will help you become ready for college and ready for a great career.

Speaking of your future, the Conversations are divided into two sections:

THINGS TO DO NOW

and

THINGS TO START THINKING ABOUT

The first section is dedicated to things you can start doing right now—today!

The second section includes important things that are on the horizon. These are things that may not be directly applicable today but you need to keep thinking about and preparing for in order to achieve academic success.

As you go through the 12 Conversations, you'll notice they are structured in four parts:

LISTEN to what the topic of Conversation is and consider why it's important.

LEARN from the examples of others we share with you.

REFLECT upon your answers to thought-provoking questions.

ACT by completing the provided action item.

Middle school is not something you have to endure or get through. It can be—in fact it should be—one of the most important times in your life. Through this guide, you can begin to lay a real foundation for success.

It is true that only you can define your own life success, but we have chosen to start with academics. Academic success unlocks the path to lifelong success. Sure, there are actually lots of paths and even more definitions of success. But we are writing about this one because it is almost a guarantee. If you do great in school, you'll have more options when you're done with school. And more options unlock more opportunities.

Now, we know you want to succeed in school. We know that you are trying really hard. How do we know? Because like we said earlier, you would not have even started this book if you didn't care. So we know that you do care. But do you ever feel like you can't get ahead? Do you sometimes feel average?

This feeling occurs because academic success is thought of as earning A's or high marks, whereas most students earn some A's but have a C average. Below is a curve that represents middle school grades in general.

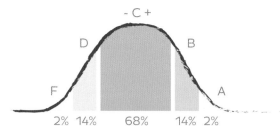

This curve is low on the left, high in the middle, and low on the right, showing you that 16% of students average F's and D's, 68% are in the middle with a C average, and another 16% of students average B's and A's.

So if you feel lost in the middle, do not worry! You're actually in really good company. But we want to help you beat the middle.

We know that grades are not the true measure of overall academic success. So we have created a list of everything you should be thinking about. Below are the 12 Conversations we will have with you and your parents/mentors that will help you achieve success.

The 12 Conversations

1. GOALS

2. PLANNING & PREPARATION

3. TIME MANAGEMENT

4. GRADE POINT AVERAGE (GPA)

5. EXTRA- & CO-CURRICULAR ACTIVITIES

6. SERVICE

7. COLLEGE ENTRANCE EXAMS

8. INTERNSHIPS & WORK EXPERIENCE

9. MONEY MANAGEMENT & SCHOLARSHIPS

10. COLLEGE APPLICATION PROCESS

11. INTERVIEWING

12. SHARE YOUR EXPERIENCE

Are you ready? Then turn the page already!

A THOUGHT
TO PONDER

"There are some folks you can talk to until you're blue in the face—they're never going to get it and they're never going to change. But every once in a while, you'll run into someone who is eager to listen, eager to learn, and willing to try new things. Those are the people we need to reach. We have a responsibility as parents, older people, teachers, and people in the neighborhood to recognize that."

—TYLER PERRY
AMERICAN ACTOR, FILMMAKER, PLAYWRIGHT,
AUTHOR, AND SONGWRITER

A Note to
PARENTS & MENTORS

IF YOU ARE A PARENT/MENTOR OF A STUDENT reading this book, thank you! You are invested in a student's academic and lifelong success, and you are clearly seeking meaningful ways to help. We believe this book will act as a guide and prepare you to do just that.

At this point, let's be honest. The majority of middle school students will not read this book alone; therefore, we invite you to read the chapters, understand the content, and hold this student account-able to the action items at the end of each Conversation.

If you force this book onto a student, it won't work. You under-stand that. Our solution to this is to help you engage your student and assist you in presenting this material in a way that will inspire him or her to *want* academic success. We can't do this for you because you know your student best, but we are confident you will understand how best to implement the materials in this book. To help you help your student(s), we have included worksheets at the end of the Conversations. They are also available for down-load at http://www.theleaderinme.org/middleschoolsuccess.

As you do this, remember these words by William Arthur Ward:

> The mediocre teacher tells.
> The good teacher explains.
> The superior teacher demonstrates.
> The great teacher inspires.

For the best result, don't tell. If you can incorporate these principles, if you can demonstrate them and inspire your student to do better because he or she sees that it has worked for *you*, you have helped shape a life for the better.

It's unfortunate that the idea of "it takes a village to raise a child" is so politically charged because it is true. Personally, many people, including spouses, children, parents, stepparents, siblings, in-laws, friends, aunts and uncles, grandparents, cousins, religious leaders, teachers, counselors, coaches, etc., have supported us and continue to support us in our academic pursuits. These people make up our village.

When we were in a scouting program, certain skills were required to earn a merit badge—a symbol representing the scout had learned and practiced a specific skill. Someone trained in his or her field taught each merit badge class. Parents/mentors can learn from this model by connecting students with those more qualified than themselves in select areas. You'll be grateful for and surprised at the talent that exists in your family, community, and even online as you work together to help your student.

Achieving success is a process. In order for you to better understand this process, we built a Student Accountability Model that depicts a student's potential path as he or she is held accountable to apply the factors/principles found within this book.

STUDENT ACCOUNTABILITY MODEL

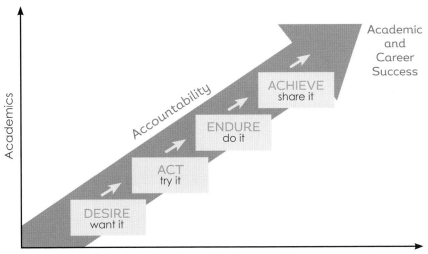

Allow us to explain this model further, but never forget that your student can achieve success! You have to believe this if he or she is going to believe it.

The Student Accountability Model is founded upon four guiding principles:

DESIRE
You *want* to succeed academically through being inspired by someone you trust.

Imagine someone giving you a delicious apple he or she grew, inspiring you to plant apple seeds and grow your own delicious apples.

ACT
You learn and *try* implementing the 12 Conversations.

You plant the apple seeds and give them water, sunlight, and nutrients. Through these actions you begin to see a plant grow—short-term evidence that what you are doing is working.

ENDURE

You consistently *do* what the 12 Conversations require over time.

 You diligently and patiently nourish the plant into a tree over a long period of time with confidence that your consistent actions will produce results—delicious apples.

ACHIEVE

You accomplish your original desire and *share* your experiences to help others achieve their potential.

 Your tree produces delicious apples you can pick, eat, and share with others who you feel would benefit and be able to grow their own delicious apples.

We've drawn arrows with each principle to represent a continuous process that:

- instills desire
- invites action
- encourages endurance
- rewards achievement over time

As you follow the four guiding principles and hold your student accountable for learning and applying the 12 factors, taught as Conversations in this book, you both will succeed, and we sincerely hope you will help others do the same.

Thank you for being supportive. Students may not always express it, but they depend on their parents/mentors for support. Students need parents/mentors who are hands-on and committed to helping them. We hope you will fulfill that role of accountability!

From this point on, we will speak directly to students because this book is for them. Let the Conversations begin . . .

A THOUGHT
TO PONDER

———• ( ) •———

"If you fail to prepare, you're prepared to fail."

—MARK SPITZ
WINNER OF 9 OLYMPIC GOLD MEDALS

CONVERSATION

1

GOALS

LISTEN. We do not expect you to make any decisions today concerning the rest of your life. That is not the purpose of this Conversation. In fact, goals change so frequently in life that it would be unrealistic to have that expectation.

We want to have a Conversation about preparing more immediate goals:

- six months
- one year
- three years
- five years

You can even make goals for a day or a week. Many people have them, but instead of calling them "goals" they simply refer to them as a "to-do" list.

So think about it.

- Where are you now?
- Where do you want to be?
- What is going to get you there?

You see, your goals are your own personal GPS navigation system. Personally, we get a little nervous leaving the house to go somewhere new without that wonderful device in our cars and on our phones that calls up directions.

Goals perform the same function. Goals keep you on the right road. Once you know where you'd like to go, goals keep you moving in the right direction.

So how do you know where you want to go? If you could sneak a peek at your future, what would make you excited? Take away all ideas of winning the lottery. Try again.

What would make you happy? What would make you proud of your future self?

Or just think about yourself right now.

- What do you love to do?
- Do you love a certain sport?
- Do you love to participate in a particular game?
- Are you a dancer?
- Are you a writer?
- Are you a reader (beyond this exact moment, of course!)?

If you could spend more time doing something, what would it be?

Do you have some ideas? We hope so, because we're going to talk about the next step. There's one extremely important concept you must know before we go even a step further. Don't worry; it's nothing new. You've probably even heard it before. *You need to write down your goals!*

One of our mentors whom we worked with closely, Dr. Stephen R. Covey, would say that a goal was not real until it was written down and you were making reasonable plans to reach the goal.

"Stop setting goals," he wrote. "Goals are pure fantasy unless you have a specific plan to achieve them."

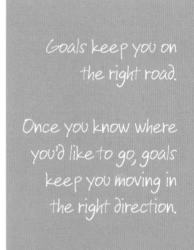

Dr. Covey refers to this as Begin with the End in Mind. In his book *The 7 Habits of Highly Effective People*, it's the second habit. If you Begin with the End in Mind, you take the time to develop an image in your mind of where or even who you want to be. Then, as you plan, you examine your choices and decisions in the context of this image. Is this part of the plan to achieve your goal? Is this going to help you get to where you want to be?

Goals keep you on the right road.

Once you know where you'd like to go, goals keep you moving in the right direction.

There is power in writing down your goals because they are direct reflections of your desires. When you write down a goal, your mind is better able to commit it to memory because it took thought and action.

There's even science to back this principle up. Even if you do not like science, you may think this is pretty cool.

A professor at the University of Oregon, Ed Vogel, is studying how our brains react when we set a goal. He's using a lot of high-tech equipment to essentially map out the brain.

He compares an efficient brain to a building that has a big guard at the door—someone who can control who comes in and who has to stay out.

If you have goals, you are able to tell your brain what can come in and what needs to go right back out. When you write down your goal your brain recognizes it and now knows that it is important.

Professor Vogel has seen that once a goal is established, a part of the brain called the globus pallidus acts as that big guard at the door. With a goal firmly established, your brain will work with you by keeping out those things that might otherwise distract you. Pretty cool, right?

So write it down and include as much detail as possible. Though, honestly, we'll take whatever you can come up with. This is not a graded assignment! So if all you have as a goal is "go to college," then we can work with that. Writing down something like "go to a top-twenty college by the time I'm nineteen years old" is, of course, a better, more defined goal, but we need to start somewhere.

You are going to have several academic goals. For example:

- earning good grades in high school
- scoring well on college entrance exams
- attending a good college

These are all great academic goals for you to consider, but be sure to consider other things.

- Do you want to play an instrument or practice a sport?
- Do you want to make a team?
- Would you like to participate in a school or community event?
- Do you want to save a certain amount of money to buy something special?

If you answered yes to any of the questions above, then make a goal. Think about how to get there. Enter your destination into your own GPS.

Now, at the beginning of this book, we talked about the importance of including a parent or mentor in this process. Remember, a parent or mentor is someone you feel that you can freely talk to about your life, your plans, and especially your goals.

Having parents/mentors included in this process has many benefits:

- First, they may recognize potential in you that you do not recognize in yourself and they can help you elevate your goals beyond what you think you can do.
- Second, they will encourage you to accomplish your goals. It's nice to have someone there to make sure you do not quit even when you get discouraged. This is too important!
- And last, but certainly not least, they have specific skills and experiences to coach you toward success.

You most likely will have a combination of parents/mentors, but having goal-specific parents/mentors to whom you are accountable is important. Give them a copy of your goals and get together as often as you need to review them.

Tell your parents/mentors why you chose them to help you. We know they will be honored to help you and will be diligent in holding you accountable for the goals you set. No matter the person, be sure you always have at least one parent/mentor with whom you check in on a weekly basis. Also, be sure this parent/mentor is honest with you about your progress.

We hope that you will also include your friends. You are old enough now that you understand the power and value of friendship. Even today, some of the most influential people in our lives are friends we made in middle school. We went through the same grades together and helped one another along the way. We know that you will do the same.

Having good friends will make you a better person. Good friends will be there for you—literally every step of the way—because they are taking the journey with you. So choose your friends and your path carefully.

We love this quote by Sean Covey. He wrote in his book *The 7 Habits of Highly Effective Teens*:

If you decide to just go with the flow, you'll end up where the flow goes, and sometimes it's headed straight downhill into a pile of sludge. You'll end up doing what everyone else is doing, which may not be your end in mind at all. "The road to anywhere is really a life to nowhere," the saying goes. You need to decide what direction feels right to you. It's really never too early.

We know that you want more than a big pile of sludge. So be willing to be picky, to want the best for your life and your future. And if that means going against the flow, so be it.

LEARN. In middle school we started a friendship with Theo. Theo struggled with obesity throughout childhood and into middle school. His weight never got to the point that he couldn't be active, but we could definitely tell he was unhappy with his appearance. At such a young age, his weight was detrimental both physically and psychologically.

This all changed one summer day. We're not sure what happened exactly, but Theo set a goal to lose weight. He was sick of the way he looked, and sick of the way he felt inside, and instead of researching intense dieting plans or quick weight-loss routines, he set a goal to run every day.

On the first day he left his house, he started his run to the nearest stop sign. Doing so nearly made him pass out, but that was his goal, and he did it! Running to the end of the street was something he had never done before, and being outdoors in front of neighbors required tremendous confidence.

With the help of his parents/mentors, Theo ran to the stop sign each day until he felt comfortable running a longer distance. Over the course of a year, Theo dropped all his extra weight and became one of the most physically fit kids in school.

In fact, Theo was able to join a competitive marching band and also became one of our high school's best cross-country runners. If you had told us in eighth grade that Theo would become one of our school's best athletes, we would not have believed you. Theo's determination is commendable, and he is proof that a young person can set and achieve major goals.

Theo's story is inspiring and is one of many examples of students who desire change and achieve it through goal-setting and hard work. We have seen family and friends overcome illness, earn high grades and test scores, build business empires, and help others through years of service to community and military organizations, to name a few.

With the resources available to us through modern research and technology, we hardly ever hear the word "impossible" anymore. Whatever your goals are, now is the time to develop them with the help of a parent/mentor.

Do not wait until you are forced to think about your future because your college application is due next week. Things will fall into place if you start now. Imagine what opportunities will open up to you when looking for a great college having already set goals and taken the necessary steps to succeed years before applying.

REFLECT. Please take as much time as you need to ponder the following questions. Then, with the help of your parents/mentors, fill in your answers in the space provided.

As you consider the questions in this conversation and the ones to follow, be sure to reference the student accountability model below. Make sure you consider how to identify your desire, list specific actions to achieve it, and ways to maintain your progress and further it by sharing, as you answer. As the arrow indicates, these steps all build on each other!

STUDENT ACCOUNTABILITY MODEL

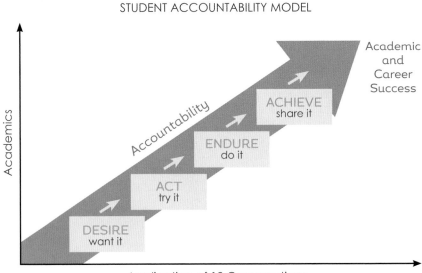

Application of 12 Conversations

What are the most important things you want to accomplish in life?

_____

_____

_____

_____

_____

_____

_____

_____

_____

_____

_____

_____

_____

_____

_____

_____

What would you like to improve in your life? What can you do to start improving today?

_____

_____

_____

_____

_____

_____

_____

_____

_____

_____

_____

_____

_____

_____

Where do you see yourself in six months? In one year? In three years? In five years?

_____

_____

_____

_____

_____

_____

_____

_____

_____

_____

_____

_____

_____

_____

_____

How often do you need to meet with your parents/mentors to review your goals?

_____

_____

_____

_____

_____

EXAMPLE

This page can be referenced as an example when filling out your own Goals Action Sheet on the following page, or by downloading the template at http://www.theleaderinme.org/middleschoolsuccess.

TOP SIX LIFELONG GOALS	PARENTS/MENTORS
1. School: Graduate from college.	Ms. Kinzer – English teacher
2. Home: Have a happy family.	My parents
3. Work: Pursue a career I love.	Aunt Swendy – entrepreneur
4. Health: Live a healthy lifestyle.	Jesse – my running partner
5. Service: Serve others daily.	Maureen – community leader
6. Fun: Enjoy life!	Sam – my best friend

GOALS

ACT. As you reflect upon the most important things in your life, please write down your top six goals and the people who will help you achieve each goal. Having lifelong goals will guide you in the years to come. Please make a copy of this action item to share with your parents/mentors. Please visit http://www.theleaderinme .org/middleschoolsuccess to download this template.

TOP SIX LIFELONG GOALS	PARENTS/MENTORS
1.	
2.	
3.	
4.	
5.	
6.	

A THOUGHT
TO PONDER

———•·•·•———

"Another way to be prepared is to think negatively. Yes, I'm a great optimist. But, when trying to make a decision, I often think of the worst case scenario. I call it 'the eaten by wolves factor.' If I do something, what's the most terrible thing that could happen? Would I be eaten by wolves? One thing that makes it possible to be an optimist, is if you have a contingency plan for when all hell breaks loose. There are a lot of things I don't worry about, because I have a plan in place if they do."

—RANDY PAUSCH
AMERICAN PROFESSOR OF COMPUTER SCIENCE,
HUMAN-COMPUTER INTERACTION, AND DESIGN AT
CARNEGIE MELLON UNIVERSITY (CMU) IN PITTSBURGH,
PENNSYLVANIA

CONVERSATION

2

PLANNING & PREPARATION

LISTEN. Now that we have gone through the process of setting goals, you need a period of reflection to plan the steps necessary to accomplish your goals and to prepare yourself for anything that could happen as you work to execute your plan.

Let's start making that plan together.

We're going to talk more about daily planning in a future Conversation dedicated to time management. For now, let's talk about how planning and preparation can help you accomplish your goals.

One successful method of organizing your planning and preparation is to think about your life in six-month increments.

Knowing what you want to do today and tomorrow and next week and next month is important, but true planning and preparation comes when you take several months at a time and set realistic benchmarks.

For us, the benchmarks that make sense are the beginning of a new calendar year and the beginning of a new school year. These dates are natural breaking points and they serve as great reflection times for what is to come in your life in the next half year, especially as it relates to your academic success.

- What are your plans for the next six months?
- Do you have any ideas?

If not, we'd like to give you a suggestion on how to come up with some ideas.

It's basically this: **Take time to think about it.**

For us, we do our best thinking in the morning.

Hopefully your morning is not a mad rush from your alarm bell to the school bell. Because if you get up a little early, when things around you are still quiet, you can tap into a great resource: meditation. A great key to academic success is setting aside time for reflection and pondering.

The process of reflection is different for each person and, though we have a bias for the morning, it actually can occur at different times of the day. Some people start their day quietly reading and writing. Others think best while exercising after school or taking a shower at night.

It does not matter how you reach this time of quiet contemplation that will help you plan your day; the important thing is that you simply reach it and reach it often.

Why?

Because life is noisy. You are surrounded by "noise" that comes from daily activities, actual environmental noise from televisions and other devices, destructive media messages, and even peers who seek to distract and demean. If you take time to quietly think, you can focus on what is really important. You can focus on your goals. You can plan how to accomplish your goals, especially your goal of academic success.

This process of reflection is also not something you do once a week. In *The 7 Habits of Highly Effective People*, Habit 7: Sharpen the Saw, Dr. Covey explained the need for meditation in our daily lives. Why? Because yesterday's meal is not going to satisfy the hunger you feel today. You need to consistently reflect, consistently meditate, and consistently plan.

Now, people have many ways of relaxing and thinking; however, allow us to share a few tips we believe can work for you.

TIP 1: Wake up early! Starting your day in reflection or meditation is a remarkable way to achieve your goals because your mind and body are alert. We could spend a lot of time showing you the hundreds of articles about this practice and how it will bring you success, but honestly, just try it, and you will realize why it is effective. Start today. Go to bed at a reasonable time and set your alarm for 6 a.m. After you wake up, spend the next hour in a set routine that consists of, but is not limited to, exercising, showering, reading, and writing. After you are done with those things, you can finish getting ready for the day and go to school. Now, we already know that some of you are thinking, "Great idea, but that's not going to happen!" Well, we invite you to try it, and we promise you will learn to love the early morning hours more than any other time of your day because of how productive you will be.

TIP 2: Make a habit of thinking through your entire day during your morning routine. What do you need to be prepared for? Who are you going to run into? Is there anything you are forgetting, or are there opportunities that you haven't thought about yet?

Life is noisy.

You are surrounded by "noise" that comes from daily activities, actual environmental noise from televisions and other devices, destructive media messages, and even peers who seek to distract and demean.

If you take time to quietly think, you can focus on what is really important.

You can focus on your goals.

You can plan on how to get there.

TIP 3: Make sure you are planning and allowing for enough time to complete your homework. Think about your schedule. How much time do you need to set aside to successfully complete your assignments?

TIP 4: Use resources to help you plan your time. You can purchase a personal planner. You can utilize a planner app for your phone. You can buy a calendar. You can set up a schedule on your computer. Choose whatever works for you. And guess what? You're young, so that means that you have lots of time to try out different things. We simply recommend that you have something where you can write down important due dates and personal to-do lists. You will think of several things during the morning and even throughout the day that you need to remember. Write them down. For example, if you know you have a presentation in your history class later in the day, and while in your morning routine you have the idea to play a certain video in your presentation, write it down. This will be a physical reminder to do it. Just like with goals, you will forget "aha" moments unless you write them down. A running to-do list is essential for you to be as productive as possible, and trust us, the majority of your best ideas will come in the early hours of the morning.

TIP 5: The last concept we want you to consider is the need to do more research while planning and preparing. Too many people decide they are going to do something without fully understanding all of the details or options. For example, when we got to the point of applying to colleges, we remember many friends simply applying to the college closest to home or to the college their family all attended. Some didn't even think about going to college after high school because nobody encouraged them to go, perhaps because many of their parents/mentors did not go themselves. Now this is just one example, but we could discuss many scenarios, such as picking which classes to take in school or where to work or what activities to get involved in. The point is this: Do your research! Take an hour to look at your options and make a pros and cons list. Planning and preparing for your life is too important to leave up to spontaneous reaction. Remember, your parents/mentors can and should assist you with your research. Just ask them for help.

LEARN. The valedictorian of our high school class (out of 800+ graduating seniors) was Bryce, and he happened to be one of our best friends. Bryce earned a perfect 4.0 grade point average (GPA) every quarter in school since the seventh grade, which means he brought home twenty-four perfect quarterly report cards before he graduated from high school!

He is an amazing individual who understands what it means to plan and prepare. Bryce also finished high school with more than sixty college credits; so in addition to his high school diploma, Bryce received his associate's degree and a scholarship to pretty much any college he wanted to attend without having to pay anything.

We can't remember a time when Bryce came to class without having a finished assignment or without having read ahead in preparation for the day's lecture.

Bryce had always been a little reserved. He wasn't a "know-it-all" student with his hand raised frequently, although he did ask questions when needed. Bryce simply understood the meaning of preparing and planning for the day. He had a routine and would think ahead.

Bryce knew in seventh grade that his hard work would pay off later, and he started to build his résumé at an early age. He researched the teachers and classes at our school to find the right fit for his talents and aspirations. Often we would find Bryce reading and in deep thought, and you could see from the absorbed look on his face that he was in full concentration mode.

Was he nerdy? Yes, a little, but that didn't mean that hobbies, friends, and fun weren't part of his life.

There's enough time for everything if you work hard and do not procrastinate. We learned a lot from Bryce about dedicating time to a goal and planning for the accomplishment of that goal. Bryce continues to teach us what it means to be smart and well-rounded. Some people are just plain gifted with intelligence, true, but you can teach yourself and learn to be smart with the right planning and preparation.

REFLECT. Please take as much time as you need to ponder the following questions. Then, with the help of your parents/mentors, fill in your answers in the space provided.

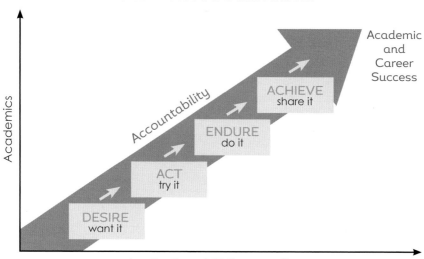

STUDENT ACCOUNTABILITY MODEL

Academics

Accountability

Academic
and
Career
Success

ACHIEVE
share it

ENDURE
do it

ACT
try it

DESIRE
want it

Application of 12 Conversations

What do you need to plan and prepare for in the next six months?

_____

_____

_____

_____

_____

_____

_____

What helps you think and reflect?

_____

_____

_____

_____

_____

_____

What resources are available to help you plan better? How can you use those resources to keep track of your goals?

_____

_____

_____

_____

_____

_____

_____

_____

How can your parents/mentors help you realize your goals?

_____

_____

_____

_____

_____

_____

_____

_____

PLANNING & PREPARATION

EXAMPLE

This page can be referenced as an example when filling out your own Planning & Preparation Action Sheet on the following page, or by downloading the template at http://www.theleaderinme .org/middleschoolsuccess.

TOP SIX LIFELONG GOALS	SIX-MONTH PLAN
1. School: Graduate from college.	• Do my homework every day. • Earn a 3.8 GPA this semester/quarter. • Visit one college campus with my parents/mentors.
2. Home: Have a happy family.	• Spend more time with my family each day. • Help with household chores. • Write in my journal weekly.
3. Work: Pursue a career I love.	• Visit two people at work to learn what they do. • Update my financial budget every week. • Read a good book from cover to cover.
4. Health: Live a healthy lifestyle.	• Exercise three times each week. • Stop eating so much sugar. • Find time to reflect/meditate daily. • Get 7+ hours of sleep per night.
5. Service: Serve others daily.	• Volunteer at a local service organization at least once a month. • Make a new friend at school. • Offer to help friends with homework.
6. Fun: Enjoy life!	• Beat my high score on my favorite game. • Join a club at school. • Play my favorite sport/instrument/activity every week.

PLANNING & PREPARATION

ACT. As you think about your six lifelong goals that you listed in the last Conversation, begin to set specific plans for the accomplishment of your goals in the next six months and continually repeat this process. Please visit http://www .theleaderinme.org/middleschoolsuccess to download this template.

TOP SIX LIFELONG GOALS	SIX-MONTH PLAN
1.	
2.	
3.	
4.	
5.	
6.	

A THOUGHT
TO PONDER

———————— ⟨•⟩ ————————

"Determine never to be idle. No person will have occasion to complain of the want of time who never loses any. It is wonderful how much can be done if we are always doing."

—THOMAS JEFFERSON
AMERICAN FOUNDING FATHER, PRINCIPAL AUTHOR OF
THE DECLARATION OF INDEPENDENCE, AND THE THIRD
PRESIDENT OF THE UNITED STATES

CONVERSATION 3

TIME MANAGEMENT

LISTEN. We truly believe time management is one of the most important factors in achieving academic success.

We all have twenty-four hours in a day. In fact, every living person has the exact same amount of time given to him or her each day. How we use it depends entirely on us.

Using it wisely is a skill. But do not worry, it is a skill you absolutely can develop—if you have not done so already.

You might hear people, especially adults, complain that there is "never enough time." We have even heard people tell us that they wish they lived years before when things were simple and everyone had more TIME.

But here's the thing. Just as we said earlier, we all have the same amount of time. But what makes it more complicated now is that we have so many options of how to fill that time.

So stop telling yourself that you do not have "any time" because it's simply not true. You just have the luxury of so many options that fight for that time.

Here's a great truth: How you spend your time shows what you truly value.

Let's break it down. You have twenty-four hours every day. Now, a lot of those you need to spend sleeping—that is crucially important—and many of them are spent in school. But outside of that, there is time which can be utilized to the fullest, and if you choose to use your time wisely, you'll have a lifelong skill that will ensure your continued success.

Use the amazing technology available to you.

Channel it into becoming a productive student now and through high school.

If you have not mastered this skill yet, we'd like to share some things that have helped us.

Put your schedule in writing. This can happen in a variety of ways, but the two most common are in a handwritten planner or an electronic calendaring system on your phone and/or computer. Choose what works best for you.

In middle school, your time may not be completely your own. Even if you don't think so, your life is busy. We know that you have a morning routine (because you were so motivated by our last Conversation), you have school with certain classes each day, you have homework, you have after-school activities, you have mealtimes, you have friends, and you have hobbies—to name a few things. You need to start putting all of this in a calendar so you are organized.

For example, at the beginning of a new school year, you get a list of expectations and assignments/quizzes/exams called an outline or a syllabus. Have you ever gone home with that syllabus and entered all the due dates into your calendar? Why not?

You need to know when things are due so they don't sneak up on you. If your science teacher has a final project due in four months, then enter it into your calendar, and if you are using an electronic calendar, set up a recurring monthly reminder. You can even go as far as scheduling time after school that says, "Work on science project." This way you are able to be at ease in class knowing that you have already taken the necessary steps to be prepared.

Also, it is important for you to map out your homework because you may have three exams in one week and not know about it until that week comes up because you didn't write them down. If you had organized your calendar in advance, then you would have expected the week coming up to be rough and would have prepared for it.

Having a robust and detailed calendar takes a lot of time, especially if this is new for you.

Don't worry.

Once you get into it, you will find planning to be quite enjoyable because you will see yourself becoming more productive. As your calendar fills up, knowing what areas of your life need improvement will be more apparent.

Use the amazing technology and resources available to you. Channel it into becoming a productive student now and through high school.

Do not forget to have fun. It's okay to purposefully schedule time to have fun. Finding a workable balance between all of your responsibilities and the things you want to do for fun will make you happier. If there is a concert in a few months or a movie you pre-bought tickets for, then put it in your calendar. You will find yourself looking forward to these types of events.

Do not get sucked into time-wasting activities. As you get more familiar with your calendar, you will discover that you indeed have more time than you think. Perhaps the most pervasive problem students face today is the overuse of technology offerings, such as gaming and social media. There comes a time when you need to turn off distractions and focus on the important tasks at hand. Nothing will cause a student to fail more than these addictive distractions. If you are not capable of doing this on your own, ask parents/mentors to intervene and help you set acceptable limits.

Many will say that every minute of every day does not need to be planned. We agree.

Of course, we all want some free time; nevertheless, having a detailed and documented calendar will allow you to foresee those times when you just need to relax.

Spontaneous activities that bring us happiness can fit into a schedule—in fact, we've even gotten to the point of planning free time into our calendar! As you become more organized, you will have more control of your time.

So break it down. Look at your day. And find out:

- When will I be in school?
- When do I need to study?
- When do I need to work/complete chores?
- When can I play?

You do not have to be a prisoner to your schedule. You are young! Use a schedule to help you, not hurt you.

We'll share an example. We have a friend whose oldest child is a really smart girl. Her teachers love to teach her; her coaches love to coach her; her friends love to play with her. You get the picture.

But she gets overwhelmed. She knows she needs to practice the piano, finish her homework, do her chores, go to soccer practice, get her reading minutes in, help the elderly cross the street, and bake cookies for the neighbors.

It's too much for her! It is too much for anyone.

She could not figure out how to do all of it, to the standard she wanted to do it, and so she retreated into a chair in her living room with a game console.

Her parents were frustrated! What was going on?

And they remembered when she was in the first grade her teacher gave her an assignment to read one hundred books in five months.

Once they broke it down, it was an achievable goal. But their daughter heard one hundred and shut down. She couldn't do it! She came home from school crying. She was going to fail!

Her parents broke it down and showed her how easy it would be to achieve this goal over twenty-five weeks. Once it was broken down, she could visualize it. She was not overwhelmed anymore.

> You do not have to be a prisoner to your schedule. You are young! Every single minute of every single day should not be and does not have to be scheduled. Use a schedule to help you, not hurt you.

They needed to do the same thing for her when she was older— break it down, show her that it was achievable.

And they did. They helped her break her day down. They helped her write time in for what she wanted to do and showed her how much time she had left that was FREE.

In this way, a schedule worked for her, not against her. Why? Because it removed the anxiety.

Developing the habit of being a great time manager is tough. When you are sitting in a meeting and someone announces an upcoming activity, you need to train yourself to pull out your calendar and put in the activity right then and there.

Don't wait. You won't remember it later.

You will also find that other people will start respecting you more because you will remember their activities and important dates, and you will be known as a person who shows up to events or at least apologizes in advance for not being available. Nothing is more annoying than someone who doesn't plan for or forgets an important event.

Don't put this off. Don't schedule a future date to be great at time management. Please start today.

LEARN. Jada is a former classmate and friend of ours who understands what it means to manage time. For about four months we were in the same classes as Jada, and we were able to witness and learn firsthand from her organizational techniques.

Over the summer before our classes even began, our teachers assigned heavy reading and writing assignments to bring to the first day of class. The accompanying assignments were not small. We're talking about fifteen books and essays! On top of this, we averaged more than four hundred pages of weekly reading and more than ten pages of writing assignments throughout the semester.

This was an intense scholarship program and truly forced us to manage our time. While many scholars experienced high levels of stress, Jada always remained calm, collected, and ahead of the class.

One specific day, we remember sitting next to Jada. She had a sort of obsession with anything Disney. Many of her school supplies were Disney-themed. Next to her Mickey Mouse calculator, Jada kept her planner, a collection of sticky notes, and various colored labels. This was a girl who definitely had a system that made sense to her, and really, that's all that mattered.

As the teacher assigned the various homework projects, Jada went to work. Each class was color-coded, and homework was highlighted and assigned a specific time, depending on the amount of homework given out. It is no wonder that Jada was prepared for every class with great comments and could summarize all of the pre-class reading, because she scheduled sufficient time to complete the assignments. Learning became enjoyable for her, and her reputation in class was so stellar that when students didn't know an answer, they would say, "I don't know, ask Jada!"

Another one of Jada's impressive qualities was her dependability. She attended every class and social event and remembered special occasions as well. For example, she remembered our birthday, which we had only mentioned once in a casual conversation. She must have quickly put it into her calendar. Now that was cool. These are the types of time-management skills that make a successful student and a reputable person.

REFLECT. Please take as much time as you need to ponder the following questions. Then, with the help of your parents/mentors, fill in your responses in the space provided.

STUDENT ACCOUNTABILITY MODEL

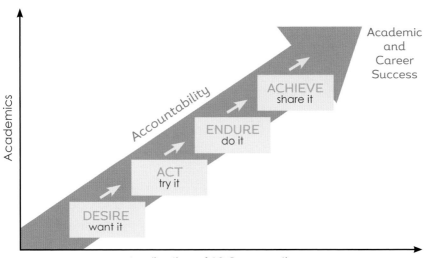

How could you better utilize your time?

_____

_____

_____

_____

_____

_____

_____

What type of planning tools are you currently using? Are there time-management devices or methods you are not utilizing?

_____

_____

_____

_____

_____

What kinds of responsibilities or events do you tend to miss often? How can better time management help you overcome this?

_____

_____

_____

_____

_____

_____

_____

Discuss with your parents/mentors the most important things in your life to make time for.

_____

_____

_____

_____

_____

_____

_____

TIME MANAGEMENT

EXAMPLE

This page can be referenced as an example when filling out your own Time Management Action Sheet on the following page, or by downloading the template at http://www.theleaderinme.org /middleschoolsuccess.

	Mon	Tue	Wed	Thu	Fri	Sat	Sun
6 A.M.–7 A.M.	Wake up, exercise, shower, get ready	Wake up, exercise, shower, get ready	Wake up, exercise, shower, get ready	Wake up, exercise, shower, get ready	Wake up, exercise, shower, get ready		
7 A.M.–8 A.M.							
8 A.M.–9 A.M.	School homework due: Biology project, Math assignment 1, and music hours sheet	School homework due: English essay draft and design for yearbook	School homework due: Math assignment 2	School homework due: final Introduction in English essay and solo competition is today in music	School		
9 A.M.–10 A.M.						Mow lawn & clean room	
10 A.M.–11 A.M.							Service
11 A.M.–12 P.M.						University campus tour	
12 P.M.–1 P.M.							
1 P.M.–2 P.M.							Nap time!
2 P.M.–3 P.M.							
3 P.M.–4 P.M.	Sports practice	Drama club	Sports practice	Drama club	Sports practice		
4 P.M.–5 P.M.		Homework		Homework			
5 P.M.–6 P.M.	Family dinner	Family dinner	Family dinner	Family dinner	Family dinner		Family dinner
6 P.M.–7 P.M.	Homework	Piano	Homework	Watch TV	Homework		
7 P.M.–8 P.M.	Family activity	Watch TV	Hang out with friends	Community activity	Volunteer	Basketball with friends	
8 P.M.–9 P.M.							Journal
9 P.M.–10 P.M.	Read and sleep	Read and sleep	Read and sleep	Read and sleep			Read and sleep
10 P.M.–11 P.M.					Read and sleep	Read and sleep	

TIME MANAGEMENT

ACT. In this section you will be taking time to thoroughly plan out an entire week. Think about everything you *must* accomplish and everything you *want* to accomplish. Refer to this calendar throughout your day and make decisions based on your plans. We encourage you to get in the habit of planning each week. Please visit http://www.theleaderinme.org/middleschoolsuccess to download this template.

	Mon	Tue	Wed	Thu	Fri	Sat	Sun
6 A.M.–7 A.M.							
7 A.M.–8 A.M.							
8 A.M.–9 A.M.							
9 A.M.–10 A.M.							
10 A.M.–11 A.M.							
11 A.M.–12 P.M.							
12 P.M.–1 P.M.							
1 P.M.–2 P.M.							
2 P.M.–3 P.M.							
3 P.M.–4 P.M.							
4 P.M.–5 P.M.							
5 P.M.–6 P.M.							
6 P.M.–7 P.M.							
7 P.M.–8 P.M.							
8 P.M.–9 P.M.							
9 P.M.–10 P.M.							
10 P.M.–11 P.M.							

A THOUGHT
TO PONDER

———•⟨⟩•———

"We are taught you must blame your father, your sisters, your brothers, the school, the teachers—but never blame yourself. It's never your fault. But it's always your fault, because if you wanted to change you're the one who has got to change."

—KATHARINE HEPBURN
AMERICAN ACTRESS

CONVERSATION 4

GRADE POINT AVERAGE (GPA)

LISTEN. Chances are that a few short years ago your grades were reported in numerical form. You would get a report card with the "grade" being a 1, 2, 3, or 4. You were not sure exactly what the number meant or even how you compared with your peers.

Now you understand. Your grades are now the traditional A's, B's, and C's, and, even more intimidating, they will soon begin to "officially count," which means they are used to compute your overall GPA. Colleges will look at them. You will be ranked because of them.

The uniqueness of this book is the fact that we are preparing you to think about college at an earlier age—before even beginning high school. One of the main reasons we are doing this is so you can start off on the right track with your grades. As we said, colleges will start counting grades at the beginning of high school, which typically starts in ninth grade; nevertheless, earning good grades before ninth grade is crucial because you begin to form your study habits and routines.

Too often we see high school juniors and seniors who have poor GPAs, and there is nothing anybody can do about it. Unfortunately, it's too late. You can't go back and change your grades as you are finishing high school, and grades are extremely important in college admissions.

Many colleges in America are trying to get to a system where they can evaluate you on much more than grades. This is called holistic admissions, and we are advocates for this movement. This approach looks at grades and test scores and involvement and diversity and overcoming hardships, etc. However, most community and public as well as private colleges still have what is called an index score for their admissions process, which is a combination of your grades and test scores.

The index score is calculated using a table like in the game Battleship. In Battleship you may say to your opponent "B5," and they go down to row "B" and over to column "5" to check and see if you have hit one of their ships.

In the case of a student who has a 3.8 GPA and a 28 ACT score; the college representative goes from a 4.0 GPA to 3.8 GPA and down from a 36 ACT to a 28 ACT, and the number found at the intersection is your index score. The higher your GPA and test score, the higher your index score. In many cases, everything from admissions to scholarship awards is based on index scores.

We often hear that grades aren't everything or some students are just naturally good at earning A's.

Well, of course grades aren't everything.

You are more than a number. We hope that you have many goals in life beyond earning good grades, but in terms of going to college, your GPA has proven to be a fairly accurate predictor of your future academic success.

You must work for good grades and also make sure you find time for outside activities.

As for those who "naturally get A's"—we don't buy it. Too often we have found that those who work the hardest earn the best grades. There are the occasional bright students who blow our minds, but even they know that it is important to work hard.

Fortunately, a high GPA does not mean you are required to be the smartest student in class, only the hardest working.

Remember, each of us has our own learning challenges, and for the more extensive cases, we would hope that your school and parents/mentors are advising you. Colleges have helpful resources as well and consider learning challenges in their application process; however, for the average student, grades and test scores are the major indicators considered in college admissions.

Learning is definitely the most important part of school. After high school your grades will get you into college, and your grades in college will keep you in college and will likely help you get a good job (especially when you are competing with many applicants—grades are an easy filter), but the day will come when you will be asked to show someone what you've learned. You may have received an A in history, but can you really explain the details of World War II?

Albert Einstein said, "Any fool can know. The point is to understand."

Colleges will start counting grades at the beginning of high school, which typically starts in ninth grade; nevertheless, earning good grades before ninth grade is crucial because you begin to form your study habits and routines.

And, we would add, the point is to be able to apply what you know and understand.

We recognize that learning is much more important than having a high GPA, but to get into the college of your choice and to land your dream job, you must place a heavy emphasis on earning good grades, which does not need to be hard.

You can do certain things to get good grades, and you can start doing them today.

TIP 1: Complete and turn in your assignments on time. All of them! It doesn't matter if you think you won't learn anything from a particular assignment, you've got to have something to turn in. Teachers will work with you if you are consistently trying to learn in class and attempting every assignment.

TIP 2: If possible, make sure to research the teachers that fit your learning style. Ask other students at your school about the teachers they've had. Do you like teachers who use a lot of group activities and visual presentations, or do you prefer a teacher who lectures while you take notes? We understand that in middle school and high school your options are limited. Sometimes there is only one teacher for a certain class and you have no choice, but occasionally you can choose; make sure you've done your research.

TIP 3: Just like we have discussed in previous chapters, be sure to schedule time for homework each day. If you didn't already do this in your weekly calendar from Conversation 3, then go back and do it.

Make sure you give yourself enough time. Maybe start with two hours each day, and if you finish early, great, but most days you will need that much time to do your assignments and read ahead for the next day. In fact, we've had some assignments that have taken more than two hours to complete; so be prepared each week to tailor your calendar to the needs of each class.

TIP 4: Do not be intimidated by the "hard" classes.
We remember that word gets around. You know which teachers will hand out the "easy A" and which ones will stretch you academically. It's a dilemma. You want to be challenged, but you want to maintain a good GPA! Here's our advice: Take classes that will challenge you. Taking easy classes may get you a high GPA, but you will regret this in the long run. The most competitive colleges look at your transcript and evaluate your GPA based on the courses you took; so don't be afraid to challenge yourself. You will learn more, and yes, it will be harder to maintain a high GPA, but believe in yourself and what you can do. If needed, get help from family, friends, other students, and tutoring services.

Be mindful that in high school you will have the opportunity to take college-level courses. These classes are great because you earn college credit without having to pay tuition. Remember the story of Bryce in Conversation 2? He had two years of college credits done while still in high school. Nevertheless, we also want to issue a word of caution here. We took several of these classes, but nothing beyond our limits. Many people we knew overloaded on college credits while in high school. They ended up sacrificing a high GPA that would have paid for their higher education through a scholarship. Make sure you know what you can realistically handle.

Getting good grades means more than just earning a good GPA. It also means that you can earn the trust of those around you.

You can think about trust like a bank account. By your age you probably have at least a little experience with bank accounts. You try to put more in, or deposit more, than you take out or withdraw, right? Or else horrible things happen. Like fees. Really expensive fees.

Without even knowing it, you have a trust account with your parents. When you promise to do something and then do it, you are making a deposit into your trust account. When you keep your word, you make a deposit. When you work hard and bring home strong grades, you make a deposit. And as these deposits grow, you will see the overall level of trust your parents have in you grow.

But if you are rude, if you are disrespectful, or if you lie and fail to keep your word, you make a withdrawal. And if the account is already empty, you are in trouble. You'll pay a fee. Naturally, it will not be financial. But it may come in the form of an earlier curfew or lost privileges.

Now, it is natural for parents/mentors to question you, but as you enter high school, try to get straight A's and B's for an entire year and see how their trust grows. It's remarkable how earning good grades will allow you more flexibility with your parents/mentors because they trust you.

The last thing we want to mention in this section is the importance of honesty. Nothing in life is worth compromising your reputation as an honest person, especially earning good grades. Cheating in school is wrong; however, we know it is tempting. As identical twins, we were tempted a few times to copy each other's answers or even switch clothes and take tests for each other! Nobody is free from having the temptation to cheat, and sometimes you can get away with it pretty easily.

Many years ago there was a dean at Vanderbilt University, Madison Sarratt, who told his students:

> Today I am going to give you two examinations, one in trigonometry and one in honesty. I hope you will pass them both, but if you must fail one, let it be trigonometry, for there are many good [people] in this world who cannot pass an examination in trigonometry, but there are no good [people] in the world who cannot pass an examination in honesty.

Don't be afraid to stand up for what is right. If you witness cheating, you have a responsibility to report it in an appropriate way. Cheating hurts everyone.

LEARN. Kelsey was a student in our same grade throughout middle school and high school. Kelsey was quite popular in her own way. She was a cute girl who loved her family, community, school, and painting. She was well-rounded and had clear goals. Kelsey also had incredible grades. She got along well with our teachers and always put an emphasis on getting homework done before doing anything else.

We remember calling Kelsey many times to plan something, and she would say something like, "Well, I won't be done with homework and dinner until after six thirty, so why don't we plan on seven?" What was even more impressive was that you could tell Kelsey wasn't saying that because her parents told her to. She just understood that her parents supported time with her friends because they saw her first dedicate time to homework and family.

As Kelsey went through high school, she continued to get good grades, which enabled her to help others. She set a good example. As high school ended, Kelsey knew she would get in to college. She applied to several institutions and was offered opportunities for admissions and scholarships to all of them. Her hard work literally paid off, and she continued to have a successful education and life.

Kelsey's story is extraordinary, but you would never know it. She never had all the attention on her, and she never wanted it. Kelsey just knew at an early age, even as early as seventh grade, that certain grades were needed to keep all her options open. Just because Kelsey's story sounds simple does not mean she didn't have obstacles. In fact, maintaining a high GPA demands many stressful nights trying to figure out a complicated math problem or finish a final paper or project. This doesn't even factor in the family struggles and friendship drama we all experience. Tears were shed and Kelsey's parents/mentors needed to step in and help at times, but in the end, her determination and honest work ethic made Kelsey the successful person she is today.

REFLECT. Please take as much time as you need to ponder the following questions. Then, with the help of your parents/mentors, fill in your responses in the space provided.

STUDENT ACCOUNTABILITY MODEL

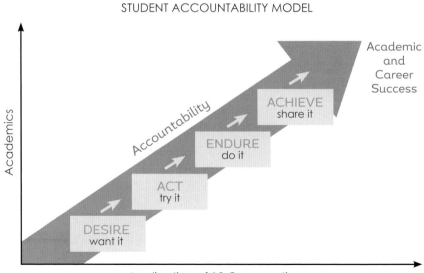

Application of 12 Conversations

Can you maintain a GPA that is higher than 3.8 (or whatever your goal is)? What do you need to meet that goal?

_____

_____

_____

_____

_____

What times and locations are best for you to do homework?

_____

_____

_____

_____

What types of classes are you most interested in taking?

_____

_____

_____

_____

_____

How often can you meet with a parent/mentor to go over your grades and study habits? Is there an online resource provided by your school that would make this process easier?

_____

_____

_____

_____

_____

_____

GRADE POINT AVERAGE (GPA)

EXAMPLE

This page can be referenced as an example when filling out your own GPA Action Sheet on the following page, or by downloading the template at http://www.theleaderinme.org /middleschoolsuccess.

GPA TRACKER

	Quarter 1		Quarter 2		Quarter 3		Quarter 4	
	GPA	CUMULATIVE GPA	GPA	CUMULATIVE GPA	GPA	CUMULATIVE GPA	GPA	CUMULATIVE GPA
7th Grade	3.7	3.7	3.8	3.75	3.9	3.8	4.0	3.85
8th Grade	3.8	3.8	4.0	3.9	3.7	3.83	3.6	3.78
9th Grade								
10th Grade								
11th Grade								
12th Grade								

ACT. Your GPA is crucial to academic success, so it is important that you routinely track it. Every three months you should write down your current GPA and your cumulative GPA (average of all GPAs). Remember, for better or worse, your cumulative GPA is tracked the entire time you are in high school (9th–12th grade) and is the GPA that colleges will evaluate you on. Please visit http://www .theleaderinme.org/middleschoolsuccess to download this template.

GPA TRACKER

	Quarter 1		Quarter 2		Quarter 3		Quarter 4	
	GPA	CUMULATIVE GPA	GPA	CUMULATIVE GPA	GPA	CUMULATIVE GPA	GPA	CUMULATIVE GPA
7th Grade								
8th Grade								
9th Grade								
10th Grade								
11th Grade								
12th Grade								

A THOUGHT
TO PONDER

———•••———

"When I was a teenager, I began to settle in to school because I'd discovered the extracurricular activities that interested me: music and theater."

—MORGAN FREEMAN
AMERICAN ACTOR, FILM DIRECTOR, AND NARRATOR

CONVERSATION 5

EXTRA- & CO-CURRICULAR ACTIVITIES

LISTEN. When we were in middle school, there was a definite emphasis on getting involved in extracurricular activities; however, there was no mention of co-curricular activities. So, what is the difference between the two?

Not too long ago, we were invited to team up with a former college professor of ours at the university we graduated from and do research on student activities. We concluded that extracurricular activities are done outside your study area because of enjoyment and a desire to be involved. Maybe you want to study business, but you like to play sports and sing, so you try out for the tennis team and join a city choir group.

A co-curricular activity is one that is directly related to an academic interest—it is part of what you like to study. For example, if you are studying business and join the business club, that would be a co-curricular activity.

As you prepare for the future, being involved and well-rounded in your extra- and co-curricular activities is important.

In our opinion, extra- and co-curricular activities are where you gain valuable experience in several key areas of happiness, including your social life, spirituality, and physical health. Try to branch out enough to include these areas in your daily and weekly routine.

We know that many doors will open up to you as you explore new clubs and community opportunities. And if it is outside of your comfort zone, even better! Never be intimidated by something just because it is new. If you are intimidated, do not let it stop you from trying.

Be sure you are connecting with others in the real world. And find time for yourself, meditation, and staying fit. Participation in various types of clubs, hobbies, and other activities sets you apart and defines your uniqueness. When you apply for college, every student will have a GPA, but not every student joins the chess club.

Having a robust résumé that includes a variety of extra- and co-curricular involvement is important because colleges and employers want to see that you have a variety of background experiences; however, be sure you are having fun. It is possible to have fun and build your experiences at the same time.

Go out and look for things that interest you and that you sincerely want to learn more about. This way you are still building your experiences, but the fact that you are enjoying yourself will drive you to learn even more and benefit from the time you are putting into it.

Also, do not just sign up for a lot of activities without dedicating quality time to them. It's easy to tell when a student has just signed up for every club on the planet and maybe attends a couple of meetings each year versus the student who sticks to one or two clubs and is actively involved in them on a weekly, if not daily, basis. If you join for the wrong reason, you may have a nice write-up for your college application, but you will not have invested the time needed to gain anything from the experience.

Furthermore, being an active participant will result in various leadership opportunities. Most clubs or sports are in need of good leaders who will help others engage in the activity as well.

Look for those opportunities, and if they don't exist, then make them happen yourself.

Become a leader in what you enjoy doing, and if there is no official club, then become the founder. Not only will you learn skills that will help you throughout your life, some colleges actually award "leadership scholarships," so this will help put you in the running, if you are ever interested in applying later.

Don't get us wrong—we have fun too! Some of our favorite "unproductive" things in middle school were movie marathons and playing Nintendo. Have you ever spent an entire afternoon/evening watching every episode of a TV series or maybe trying to pass levels in a video game? Maybe you spend too much time worrying about your social media. Whatever the case may be, you know what tempts you and what needs to be controlled, and if you do not, your parents/mentors can probably name a few things! You can have fun and be productive—the two are not mutually exclusive of each other! We have wonderful memories of playing sports together, spending time with friends, and even finding ways to have fun doing homework and studying.

> Never be intimidated by something just because it is new. If you are intimidated, do not let it stop you from trying.

LEARN. During our freshmen year of college, we had the opportunity to interact with many students who had been very involved in extra- and co-curricular activities throughout middle school and high school. One of those students, a dear friend of ours, is named Brandon. Anybody who knew Brandon in college, and many did, knew that he was a loyal friend and a fantastic student leader.

Throughout middle school and high school, Brandon was involved in student government, event planning, marketing clubs, and several personal hobbies. He had many friends and a busy social schedule to juggle. These experiences helped Brandon apply for and receive a prestigious college scholarship that was meant for highly social and involved students. Basically, Brandon paid for his entire bachelor's degree doing what he already enjoyed doing—being proactively involved in school activities and events while encouraging others to do the same.

We enjoyed watching Brandon throughout college because his drive and passion for marketing, Web design, and sales grew in the classroom, and his social and leadership skills were developed outside of class through his scholarship and other student-involvement groups.

The best thing about Brandon is that his involvement did not stop once his schooling was paid for. He enjoys being involved so much that the art of staying busy and actively engaged has continued on throughout college and even into his career as a university recruiter, making him a respected and successful professional who is fun to be around. Even to this day, Brandon looks for opportunities to grow and develop himself in his career. The habits that were formed at an early age have only gained strength over the years and made Brandon into one of the most successful and high-spirited people we know.

REFLECT. Please take as much time as you need to ponder the following questions. Then, with the help of your parents/mentors, fill in the responses in the space provided.

STUDENT ACCOUNTABILITY MODEL

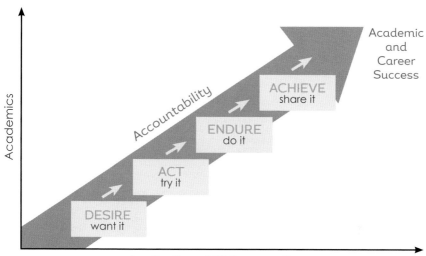

What types of extracurricular activities interest you? What types of co-curricular activities interest you?

_____

_____

_____

_____

_____

_____

_____

_____

What do you like to do for fun? Is there a club/team you could join that corresponds with this activity?

_____

_____

_____

_____

_____

_____

_____

Do you have an idea about what you want to study in college and what you want your career to be? Do any clubs/teams support this interest?

_____

_____

_____

_____

_____

_____

_____

Take the time to discuss with a parent/mentor the time-wasting activities that most tempt you. What can you replace them with?

_____

_____

_____

_____

_____

_____

_____

_____

_____

EXTRA- & CO-CURRICULAR ACTIVITIES

EXAMPLE

This page can be referenced as an example when filling out your own Extra- & Co-Curricular Activities Action Sheet on the following page, or by downloading the template at http://www .theleaderinme.org/middleschoolsuccess.

EXTRACURRICULAR ACTIVITIES

	Description	Name/Contact	Meeting Times
Activity #1	Member of school sports team	Coach Matthews cell phone: (xxx) xxx-xxxx	Mondays, Wednesdays, and Fridays from 3-5 P.M.
Activity #2	Take piano lessons each week	Lori cell phone: (xxx) xxx-xxxx	Tuesdays at 6:30 P.M.

CO-CURRICULAR ACTIVITIES

	Description	Name/Contact	Meeting Times
Activity #1	Practicing to become an actress	Mr. Johnson mjohnson@email.edu	Tuesdays and Thursdays from 3-4 P.M.
Activity #2	Receive support in hard classes	Mrs. Kinzer skinzer@email.edu	Anytime during school or by appointment

EXTRA- & CO-CURRICULAR ACTIVITIES

ACT. The template provided in this section requires you to fill out two extracurricular activities and two co-curricular activities that describe your interests. These activities can include clubs, hobbies, professional organizations, etc. Take some time to fill in the activities you are currently involved in and/or would like to be involved in. Write a short description of the activity, the name and contact information of the person in charge, and a list of meeting times to put into your weekly calendar. Please visit http://www.theleaderinme.org/middleschoolsuccess to download this template.

EXTRACURRICULAR ACTIVITIES

	Description	Name/Contact	Meeting Times
Activity #1			
Activity #2			

CO-CURRICULAR ACTIVITIES

	Description	Name/Contact	Meeting Times
Activity #1			
Activity #2			

A THOUGHT
TO PONDER

— • ⟨•⟩ • —

*"Life's most persistent and urgent question is,
'What are you doing for others?'"*

—DR. MARTIN LUTHER KING JR.
AMERICAN BAPTIST MINISTER, ACTIVIST, HUMANITARIAN,
AND LEADER IN THE CIVIL RIGHTS MOVEMENT

CONVERSATION 6

SERVICE

LISTEN. Several decades ago during the World War II holocaust, one of our heroes, Viktor Frankl, was imprisoned and starving. He was a slave laborer in a concentration camp.

You need to understand that Frankl was brilliant. He studied both neurology and psychiatry in Vienna, Austria. However, that did not matter as much to his captors as the fact that he was Jewish.

Instead of wallowing in despair over his unfair treatment, Frankl took his observations and wrote a book, *Man's Search for Meaning*, which has changed the lives of millions.

You see, while he was in the concentration camps, he noticed that there were some people who were not only surviving, they were thriving. These people refused to lose themselves—refused to lose their souls—because of their horrific circumstance. They still loved others. They still served others. He wrote about what he was observing. The Nazis found his notes and burned them. So he started over and wrote about how we all need to have meaningful projects, to perform acts of service, and to make a difference in order to strengthen our lives.

Upon reflection on our own experiences, we noticed that service has played a major part in two ways:

- First, service is what others were doing for us as our parents/mentors.
- Second, service is the key component to understanding true leadership and thus is an important part of what colleges and universities want to see in your background.

Allow us to talk about both of these points further.

There is a concept in the universe known as collective thinking or karma. Whatever you may call it, there is power in "thinking happy thoughts" and "what goes around comes around."

We are firm believers that you must recognize the service others are doing on your behalf and give them the appropriate gratitude and, at the same time, look for ways to serve those around you. Pay it forward. Use the talents you have and look for ways to help others.

One of our professors in college and perhaps one of the most influential mentors in our lives is Lynne. In one of Lynne's classes, we participated in an activity where we drafted a Personal Mission Statement.

If you take the time to complete a Personal Mission Statement, it is truly a soul-searching, deeply introspective activity because this type of statement is meant to be a statement, or series of statements, that defines your life's mission.

A mission statement explains who you want to be, what you want to do, and the values you have that will help you get there. It's your own personal motto.

For example, a part of your Personal Mission Statement may say:

- I am kind and respectful to those around me by acknowledging their worth and individual talents.
- My actions live up to my beliefs.
- I do not ask others to change so that I can be happy; I seek to be the change I need.

As you grow, your Personal Mission Statement will grow with you. Sean Covey wrote in his book *The 7 Habits of Highly Effective Teens*:

A Personal Mission Statement is like a tree with deep roots. It's stable and it's not going anywhere, but it's also alive and continually growing. Standing like a tree with deep roots helps you survive all of the storms of life that beat you up. As you've probably noticed already, life is anything but stable. Think about it. People are fickle. Your boyfriend loves you one minute and then dumps you the next. You're someone's best friend one day, and they're talking behind your back the next. . . . While everything about you changes, a Personal Mission Statement can be your deep-rooted tree that never moves. You can deal with change if you have an immovable trunk to hold on to.

In our class, we started the process of creating a Personal Mission Statement by discussing the true meaning of leadership. During our conversation, many students gave the obvious and true qualities of a leader—motivating, accomplished, driven, etc., but the conversation soon turned to service as a defining component of leadership.

When Lynne shared his Personal Mission Statement, we felt its power. It was sincere, direct, and selfless. Lynne's statement read something like this:

I will live my life helping others recognize their full potential.

What a statement of service and leadership! If you can understand this concept now at such a young age, then you will truly live an accomplished life.

Service to others is important, and the types of service discussed so far are the most important. Nevertheless, you may need to seek various types of organized service opportunities to highlight on your résumé and your college application and even to graduate because some schools require hours of service.

When you get ready to apply for college, you will see that the application process almost always requires completing a few essays. Your acts of service lend themselves to great college essays because you learn so much about yourself.

When we went through the application process, we thought we just needed to list things that related to service, no matter our involvement.

For example, our father received a heart transplant and, as a result, his story was used in various marketing campaigns in Utah, especially because at that time Miss Utah was also promoting organ donation. We were able to attend a few events and even had an opportunity to speak once. We could have written that we acted as keynote public speakers for the promotion of organ donation. But it is important to be honest. There is a big difference between saying that you helped once at an event and saying that you are a public speaker for the promotion of organ donation.

If there is a cause you want to support, such as organ donation in this example, then go out and get involved. Become the leader at your school with campaigns and fund-raisers. Having a sincere desire to serve a certain type of person, group, or cause is the ultimate motivation for real service.

Just as with extra- and co-curricular activities, have fun doing it. Service will bring about the most enjoyable experiences life has to offer you, and an important side benefit is you are improving your life experiences.

College-admissions representatives understand the meaning of true service. Time commitment and a passion to help will shine on your résumé, so make sure to have your focus in those areas rather than just a few events that you helped with one time. If you need help finding and joining organized service opportunities, ask your parents/mentors to guide you. You will be surprised at the infinite number of opportunities available to you at your school, in your community, and even on national and international levels.

LEARN. We want to tell you about David, our uncle. He is a doctor whose life has been a pathway of service. When David was in middle school and high school, he was very kind and was the first to help a friend, a family member, or anybody in need.

At the age of nineteen, David decided to take a break from his regular life of family and school to serve as a humanitarian volunteer. He spent this time in the Philippines helping others. As a volunteer, he did not have a cell phone or access to the Internet or even television.

When David returned from the Philippines, he decided to continue his education and prepare for medical school. He desired to attend a military medical school sponsored by the United States Air Force. David studied very hard to become a doctor of emergency medicine while also serving as a captain in the Air Force and raising a family.

David is truly a great example of a person who serves others as a volunteer, a member of the military, a doctor, and a family man. Each day he is saving lives one at a time. David lives a happy life because of the service he gives.

Can you imagine what our world would be like if every one of us followed in David's footsteps?

David was very smart in the way he set his goals—using the benefits of serving in the military to put himself through school. Do not underestimate what can come into your life when you put the needs of others before your own.

REFLECT. Please take as much time as you need to ponder the following questions. Then, with the help of your parents/mentors, fill in your responses in the space provided.

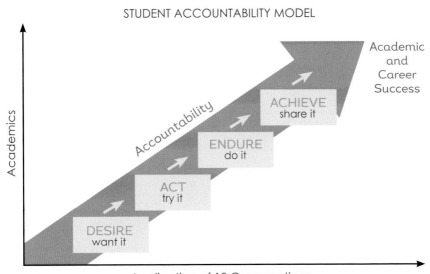

STUDENT ACCOUNTABILITY MODEL

Application of 12 Conversations

Are there certain people and/or groups that you would like to serve?

_____

_____

_____

_____

_____

What clubs or organizations would you want to join or start that revolve around service?

_____

_____

_____

_____

How can you make service a priority?

_____

_____

_____

_____

Take the time to discuss with a parent/mentor what types of activities are taking you away from being able to serve others. How can you address this together?

_____

_____

_____

_____

EXAMPLE

This page can be referenced as an example when filling out your own Service Action Sheet on the following page, or by downloading the template at http://www.theleaderinme .org/middleschoolsuccess.

MY PERSONAL MISSION STATEMENT
Write down your own Personal Mission Statement and keep it in a place where you can read it each day.

Each day I will live my life in a way that inspires others to achieve their full potential.

ACT. Now is the time for you to write your own Personal Mission Statement. Put serious thought into what you write. We encourage you to put this in a place where you can read it daily and reflect upon the words you've written. Please visit http://www .theleaderinme.org/middleschoolsuccess to download this template.

MY PERSONAL MISSION STATEMENT
Write down your own Personal Mission Statement and keep it in a place where you can read it each day.

Things to Start Thinking About

Let's transition here.

Though we've written this book for students in middle school, we actually do not know how old you are.

Are you just starting out? Or are you actually a little bit older?

We don't know.

Well, no matter your age, keep reading. But realize that if you are in middle school, some of the next few Conversations may not apply directly to you right now. But you need to think about them. You need to watch out for them, so when they do apply directly to you, you'll be ready. And you'll be successful academically and in life.

If you're a little older, the next few Conversations are exactly for you. Jump into the next six Conversations and start establishing your own path to success!

A THOUGHT
TO PONDER

———— ◦ (((◦ ————

"The price of success is hard work, dedication to the job at hand, and the determination that whether we win or lose, we have applied the best of ourselves to the task at hand."

—VINCE LOMBARDI
AMERICAN FOOTBALL PLAYER, COACH, AND EXECUTIVE

CONVERSATION 7

COLLEGE ENTRANCE EXAMS

LISTEN. Have you heard the saying "There are two sides to every story"? Well, we have found this is the case with college entrance exams.

Most students believe they are truly poor test takers. This belief occurs because we, as humans, get nervous and anxious when we are put under pressure to recite things from memory. Tests can be misleading because some people really know the information, but their nerves get the best of them.

The other side of the story is that tests are an excellent way to demonstrate knowledge. With the right amount of preparation and studying, you can be a good test taker. The GPA of a student may show ability to do homework and work hard over time, but a test really shows what an individual knows at one moment in time.

We could go back and forth about this issue, but the fact of the matter is you need to know how to test well because it not only affects your GPA, but it also affects the types of schools you can attend and how much scholarship money will be available to you.

There are two main college entrance exams. The first is the ACT (www.act.org) and the second is the SAT (www.sat.org).

Often colleges do not care which one you take because they are comparable in content and level of difficulty. Typically, where you live will determine which test is available for you to take. Each test is structured to measure your knowledge in subjects such as English, reading, writing, mathematics, science, etc. If you want to learn more about the details of these exams, we encourage you to visit their websites and seek help from your parents/mentors and school counselors.

The biggest mistake you can make with the ACT or SAT is not taking it early enough. Some states are now requiring all high school students to take the test during their junior year. This is awesome, but why was it necessary to make it mandatory?

Because not enough students were preparing for and taking the exam early! Don't be that student. In our opinion, you should plan now to test at least three times BEFORE your senior year of high school. Practice makes perfect. If you want to learn how to sing, then you don't sing the song for the first time on the night of a performance, right? Taking a test is a talent that must be practiced.

Keep practicing.

Keep trying.

Don't give up.

When the time is right, commit yourself to studying hard for this crucial exam. And keep your personal commitment.

Yes, it's just a commitment that you keep to yourself. Perhaps no one but you and hopefully your parents/mentors will know about it, but that can be the most important kind of commitment. Dr. Stephen R. Covey called those personal commitments that are kept "Private Victories." If you make and keep a personal commitment to yourself, it is a Private Victory. You are developing personal integrity; you are learning that you are someone who can follow up on and achieve personal goals; you are preparing for a brilliant future.

Preparing for the ACT/SAT includes scheduling time to study and registering for the test in advance to give yourself a deadline.

Your school will help you. Many wonderful study aids are available to help you. Utilize all that you can get your hands on! Your school will have resources you can borrow for free. Use them! Free online resources are available to you as well, and your parents/mentors can help you access these through the websites provided previously. The fact of the matter is, you have access to practice tests and questions starting now so that you can see where your weaknesses are and you can study in order to get stronger in those areas.

Scheduling time to study for the ACT/SAT is as important as your GPA; so when you have a night with no homework scheduled, use that time to study for the exam.

Chances are that studying will also help you with your classes. In fact, if you are strategic, you can coordinate topics on the exam with what you are learning in class.

For example, if you are in a geometry class learning about finding the area of various shapes, then you can bet this is in the mathematics section of the ACT/SAT.

As mentioned earlier, be sure to give yourself a deadline for taking practice exams and the actual ACT/SAT exam. You can go online and see all the dates for when the exam will be administered. Pick one as a deadline, register for it, and put it on your calendar. If the first time you take it does not go well, you can always take it more than once. In fact, most colleges will allow you to submit up to twelve different college entrance exams. Set a goal of taking the tests several times, and be sure your goal also includes setting a desired score that is tough but realistic for your abilities. We believe that scoring higher on college entrance exams is definitely the most underutilized way to pay for school. Many scholarships are out there waiting for you.

Before you start the process, take the time to research how much the test will cost. Talk to your parents/mentors about how many times it may be realistic for you to take the exam. If you get a scholarship because of your great score, it may be well worth the investment.

You should plan now to test at least three times BEFORE your senior year of high school. Practice makes perfect. If you want to learn how to sing, then you don't sing the song for the first time on the night of a performance, right? Taking a test is a talent that must be practiced.

LEARN. Okay, so this is Blake writing now. I want to use Bo's experience in this part of the book because of what he did with the ACT exam.

Bo and I both knew we wanted to go to Utah State University (USU). It was far enough from home for us to be independent, yet close enough to drive home if we needed to. We both love tennis and were offered the opportunity to play for the USU team. This was an amazing experience, but it did not come with enough funding to cover four years' worth of tuition. In order to pay for our schooling, we researched other scholarships and found an on-campus leadership program that fit our talents and paid full tuition; however, Bo did not quite have the ACT score to apply for this scholarship.

I will never forget what Bo did. He was so determined to get his education paid for that he locked himself away and studied for weeks at a time. He registered for every ACT exam available that year and, in addition, took the ACT a few more times on Utah State's campus because it was offered to prospective students with the condition that the score could only be used at USU, which was fine for Bo. In the end, Bo took the ACT nine times! He finally reached his goal, and the scholarship covered tuition and fees for up to four years. Our gratitude for such scholarship programs cannot be described in words because it was our path to a higher education.

Maybe you can relate. If so, follow Bo's example and get the score you need.

REFLECT. Please take as much time as you need to ponder the following questions. Then, with the help of your parents/mentors, fill in your responses in the space provided.

STUDENT ACCOUNTABILITY MODEL

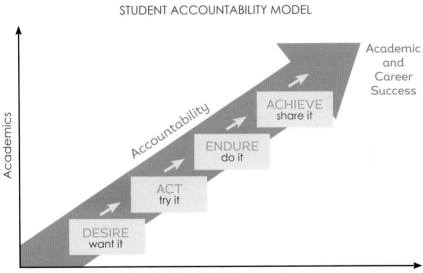

Application of 12 Conversations

What kind of score would you need to get a scholarship at the colleges near your home or at the colleges you want to attend?

_____

_____

_____

_____

_____

_____

When can you make regular time to study for the ACT/SAT?

_____

_____

_____

_____

_____

_____

What would stand in your way of scoring above the 90th percentile on the college entrance exam(s)? What is holding you back?

_____

_____

_____

_____

_____

_____

How will your parents/mentors help you study for the ACT/SAT? Who can you talk to about his/her experience taking the ACT or SAT?

_____

_____

_____

_____

_____

_____

_____

_____

_____

_____

_____

_____

COLLEGE ENTRANCE EXAMS

EXAMPLE

This page can be referenced as an example when filling out your own College Entrance Exams Action Sheet on the following page, or by downloading the template at http://www.theleaderinme.org /middleschoolsuccess.

COLLEGE ENTRANCE EXAMS

	Practice Test 1		Practice Test 2		Practice Test 3		Practice Test 4	
	MONTH	SCORE	MONTH	SCORE	MONTH	SCORE	MONTH	SCORE
9th Grade	June	17	Sept.	20	Feb.	19	March	19
10th Grade	July	21	Oct.	23	April	23	April	23
11th Grade	July	23	Sept.	24	March	25	March	26
12th Grade	June	27	July	27	August	28	Sept.	29

COLLEGE ENTRANCE EXAMS

ACT. Both the ACT and SAT exams require practice, like playing an instrument or a sport. The chart below allows you to track when you take practice exams. Our suggestion is that you take the real exam at least three times before your senior year of high school and take at least three practice exams before each real exam. If you are not happy with your score by the time you start your senior year, then you will want to take the exam as many times as you need to until you are satisfied. Please visit http://www .theleaderinme.org/middleschoolsuccess to download this template.

COLLEGE ENTRANCE EXAMS

	Practice Test 1		Practice Test 2		Practice Test 3		Practice Test 4	
	MONTH	SCORE	MONTH	SCORE	MONTH	SCORE	MONTH	SCORE
9th Grade								
10th Grade								
11th Grade								
12th Grade								

A THOUGHT
TO PONDER

———— •\|{}• ————

"The only source of knowledge is experience."

—ALBERT EINSTEIN
GERMAN-BORN THEORETICAL PHYSICIST

CONVERSATION 8

INTERNSHIPS & WORK EXPERIENCE

LISTEN. When he was a really young man, Abraham Lincoln tried out a few different careers. His father was a farmer. But apparently, his father's path was not for him. He just did not like it.

So he tried being a postmaster. And he worked as a land surveyor. He worked as a state legislator for a while. He even owned a partnership in a store.

It was while he was working in the store that a customer tried to sell a barrel to Lincoln. Lincoln did not really need another barrel, but he was kind, so he bought it. Later he dumped out the contents and found a series of law books at the bottom of the barrel. Lincoln was a store owner in an area that was populated with about fifteen cabins. He had a lot of time on his hands. So he read those books. He devoured them. And he found a new direction for his life.

Picking a career is not easy. Just like Lincoln, you may venture down several paths before you find the right fit for you. The important thing is to have a goal not only to be employed one day, but to have a job in a career you enjoy.

This Conversation on internships and work experience is a very important piece of the puzzle. To land a great career, you must have experience in jobs and internships. That experience simply will help you open the right doors and meet the right people.

Right now you might feel your opportunities are limited. And in many ways, your feelings are right. First, you're not old enough to work. State laws may require you to be in high school. Even then, you may not be able to work on a school night, depending on which state you live in and what the labor law is. Also, you are not old enough to drive, so you might be limited to opportunities close to home.

But do not tune us out quite yet. There is so much you can do right now.

- Ask around at school. They may have a program where you can job-shadow a career.
- Your school may be able to introduce you to someone already working in your dream career.
- You may be able to spend some time at a job site so that you can see what a real day at work in that career looks like. It will either strengthen your desire or perhaps set you on another path.

This is invaluable. We have a young friend who is currently a high school senior. A few years ago if you had asked him what he wanted to be when he grew up, he would have confidently answered: "Doctor!" He was smart. Really, really smart, and that is what smart kids do, right?

Well, luckily, not always. Our friend had an opportunity to job-shadow through a community health program and changed his path immediately. Guess what he discovered? He passed out at the sight of blood, even if it was not his own. No, it was time to look in a different direction.

So look around. And be aware that there are differences between working at a job and working as an intern.

A job is something you are paid to do, and you are usually expected to continually do that job unless you quit or are fired. On the other hand, an internship is a joblike experience that is set up for a specific amount of time, such as three months, six months, or whatever is agreed upon. An internship can be paid or unpaid, depending on the arrangement.

Honestly, not many internships are paid internships. On one hand, it's really too bad because you are not paid for all of your work. On the other hand, people are more willing to hire interns because they are free! And when it comes time to look for a paying job, you already have work experience on your résumé. An unpaid internship may not help your bank account in the short term, but in the long term you will find that it was absolutely worth it.

Working a job and completing internships as a student is becoming more and more common. Although some people may see this as a bad thing because you should be studying, we are of the opinion you can do both. You should seek these types of experiences because they offer several important benefits, including the valuable experience you gain from being around professionals, the work ethic you learn, and the additional income you could earn.

As we mentioned earlier, some schools even have internship programs worked into their curriculum. Ask around and see what you can find. You may have access to a program through your school. They may ask what you are interested in and help set up an internship for you.

> Picking a career is not easy.
>
> Just like Lincoln, you may venture down several paths before you find the right fit for you.
>
> The important thing is to have a goal not only to be employed one day, but to have a job in a career you enjoy.

Particularly if it is through the school, you will probably not be paid. But the most valuable lesson we can help you understand during this Conversation is the idea that volunteering for an unpaid internship can be one of the most strategic and rewarding things you ever do. It will give you an opportunity to figure out what you like to do and what you are good at. This experience will certainly help your résumé. And hopefully you will meet the people who are already working in your dream job. You can ask them how they did it. You can ask them for advice. Do not limit yourself by targeting only paid opportunities or "official" internships.

For example, let's say you want to be a graphic designer someday, but you don't have the credentials to land a job as a designer yet because you are still learning. You may easily be able to go down the street to every store or company in your neighborhood and get a job doing something else, but what if you walked into the best design firm in your town and volunteered for their team? Almost every time we've tried this, it has worked because there is no downside—the company gets free help, and you will gain career-specific experience. Also, you will develop relationships that will lead to future references and letters of recommendation for jobs and college admissions. It's a win-win situation.

How do you start the process?

- The best first step in gaining internship and work experience is an in-person meeting. Make sure you set up an appointment and go in looking like a professional with a ready résumé and a positive attitude. Just because you are young and willing to volunteer your time doesn't mean you shouldn't be impressive—you will be working on important projects; and many times an unpaid internship, if done well, can turn into a paid internship or even a job.
- If an in-person meeting is not going to work out because of the person's schedule, then writing a professional e-mail is very appropriate. Keep it short and to the point. Attach your résumé and compliment the company's successes— after all, you are impressed with them; if you weren't, you wouldn't want to work there, right?

- Do your research so that you can talk intelligently about the company. Your interest in their work can result in their interest in you.
- Be genuine in your request and discuss ways you will contribute to the company's successes.
- Request a follow-up phone conversation or an in-person meeting to discuss the opportunity further. This is the process we have used in the experiences on our résumés. It works well.

Many times we had a volunteer internship experience along with a regular job. We remember shadowing professionals in businesses, hospitals, and law firms while, at the same time, we were making a little bit of money as tennis instructors, basketball referees, lifeguards, waiters, etc.

This may be the case for you too, and if it is, then do not worry—it can be done.

All of these jobs teach you something. We learned to value working with kids, teaching others new skills, and serving people—qualities that come in handy each day of our lives. Remember, as we mentioned earlier in the book, make sure you are documenting all of these experiences, both the internships and the paid jobs.

If internships and work experiences start to take away from your academic success, then it's time to scale back. Your main focus should be school. The experiences are great and necessary but not at the expense of your grades.

Make sure you are always using the services available to you when it comes to looking for internship and work experiences. Family and friends are good places to start. Also, there are many services at your school and in the community that connect people, even young people, with great opportunities.

Be aware of opportunities you can provide for others. You may have an uncle who runs a company that you have no interest in, but maybe your friends do, or someone you know who may be looking for a job could benefit from your telling them about your uncle's business. You never know how you can change another person's life through connecting them to internship and work experiences. And, as we discussed earlier, what goes around, comes around.

Looking and acting professionally in all settings is important. Many companies will look you up online; if you haven't ever looked yourself up online, then we suggest you do it. See what you can find out about yourself as if you were the one doing the hiring.

Are there any unprofessional pictures of you that you find online?

How about the way you write and express yourself to others?

When you apply for jobs, you are basically putting yourself out there to be noticed, and people will see your name and look you up, which is easy to do these days. They will also ask others about you, so it is very important to be a kind person who remains professional in the way you present yourself both online and in person.

LEARN. Sam is our cousin, and ever since we can remember, even before middle school, he would come up with ideas to make extra money. It all started out with our boyhood club, BB&S (Bo, Blake, and Sam). Whether it was routine yard work or washing someone's boat, we did all kinds of jobs. This work ethic stuck with Sam throughout middle school and high school. He worked many jobs to support himself, such as busing tables, making sandwiches, and watching children at a daycare. He also worked at two car washes and a hearing-aid company.

As for an internship, Sam was in love with the idea of working for a professional sports team, specifically the Utah Jazz basketball team. Sam has been a Jazz fan his entire life, and one day he finally realized the opportunity had come to work with the team. Sam's family had just moved into a new neighborhood where a neighbor down the street worked with the Jazz organization. Sam was professional and up-front about his desire to work with the team and even volunteered to shadow his neighbor at work. Their relationship grew into a friendship, and Sam had many meaningful experiences with the team and the general management of the organization.

After graduating from high school, Sam received many letters of recommendation for future jobs and internships that were written by people who worked for the team. Sam decided to pursue higher education and is currently working on a bachelor's degree in order to further his career. He wants to be a lawyer.

In addition to studying, Sam is working and interning part-time. We have no doubt that upon graduation, Sam will be able to take his diploma, coupled with his vast amount of internship and work experience, and start a wonderful career.

REFLECT. Please take as much time as you need to ponder the following questions. Then, with the help of your parents/mentors, fill in your responses in the space provided.

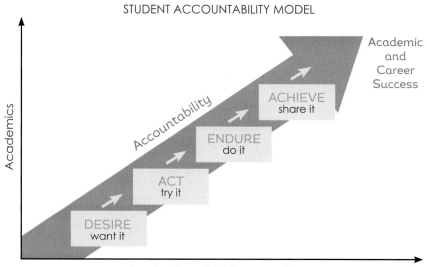

STUDENT ACCOUNTABILITY MODEL

Application of 12 Conversations

What does the ideal career look like to you?

_____

_____

_____

_____

_____

_____

What internship and work experience do you want to have? Do you know someone who could use your help with a job or an internship?

_____

_____

_____

_____

_____

_____

_____

How many hours each week would you be able to work and/or dedicate to an internship?

_____

_____

_____

_____

Do you have family, friends, and/or neighbors who can help you get a job or an internship?

_____

_____

_____

_____

_____

_____

INTERNSHIPS & WORK EXPERIENCE

EXAMPLE

This page can be referenced as an example when filling out your own Internships & Work Experience Action Sheet on the following page, or by downloading the template at http://www .theleaderinme.org/middleschoolsuccess.

RÉSUMÉ TEMPLATE	
Education	Riverton High School Riverton, Pennsylvania 3.9 GPA
Professional Experience	1. Helped my uncle in the summers teaching tennis lessons. 2. Worked for the family business on some weekends from 2010 to 2014. 3. Interned with neighbor, Swendy, at her daycare from June to December, 2013.
Leadership and Service	Captain of sports team — 9th grade Volunteer at pet shelter — once a week Community service
Honors and Awards	Most improved player for soccer 2nd place in piano recital
Professional Organizations	National Honor Society — >3.75 GPA during 7th through 9th grade
References	Aunt Swendy, coach, English teacher . . .

INTERNSHIPS & WORK EXPERIENCE

ACT. As you gain more experience and look toward future employment opportunities, you should always be aware of items that could be placed on your résumé. As you have various internship, job shadows, and work experiences, you should be writing them down on a template such as the one we're providing. We have split the template into sections to get you thinking about everything you will need on a good résumé. This is an evolving document that should be constantly updated. Please visit http://www.theleaderinme.org /middleschoolsuccess to download this template.

RÉSUMÉ TEMPLATE	
Education	
Professional Experience	
Leadership and Service	
Honors and Awards	
Professional Organizations	
References	

A THOUGHT

TO PONDER

•———•⟨|⟩•———•

"My mom played tennis for, like, six hours a day and went to college on a tennis scholarship, because that was the way she could go to school. So they [my parents] instilled in me the idea that you have to work hard for the things you want in life and never complain."

—DAKOTA FANNING
AMERICAN ACTRESS

CONVERSATION 9

MONEY MANAGEMENT & SCHOLARSHIPS

LISTEN. Unless you are a multimillionaire teenager, we know that you are broke. Really broke. Mom-can-I-get-a-loan-so-I-can-pick-something-from-the-snack-machine broke.

Money management is for everybody. It's for people who do not want to worry about money.

The key is building a budget, even if you only have $25 from Grandma to budget. We love the quote from John C. Maxwell: "A budget is telling your money where to go instead of wondering where it went."

That $25 you got from Grandma for your birthday last year—do you ever wonder where it went and why it went so fast? That does not change when you get older. That does not change simply because you have a job and you are making more money. It only makes the loss that much worse.

If you develop money-management skills now, you'll hopefully eliminate from your future a lot of the money-related stress that plagues adults.

If we could help you understand only three principles of money management, they would be:

- Do not spend more money than you make.
- Be sure to set aside money for savings.
- Be willing to give.

We know that many people have found success with what is called the "envelope system" of budgeting. Under the envelope system of budgeting, you set aside envelopes that reflect your needs:

- money for savings
- money for expenses such as clothes and entertainment
- money to donate and give

When you're filling out the loan applications, the money may seem almost like Monopoly money— almost unreal because it just shows up after the loan application is done.

Magic!

Let us assure you that paying it back is far from magical.

You can discuss budgeting with your parents/mentors and decide on an appropriate percentage to put in each envelope.

The beauty of the envelope method is that once the money is gone, it is gone. The envelope method teaches you to be careful with your purchases and eliminates the opportunity for debt spending and reliance on credit cards. But if you are ready for the next level, take the time to open a savings account and a checking account, and find opportunities to give to your community, or even worthy causes throughout the world.

As we discussed earlier in the book, you should seek

opportunities to be a volunteer intern; however, you are more than likely going to need a job or some other means of making some money, especially as you get older.

This is how it is for most families, including our own, during middle school and high school. Our guess would be that your parents/mentors do not have extra money to throw your way, and even if they did, they shouldn't because you need to learn how to earn it.

Even if you are struggling financially, you can find ways to get back on track through hard work and wise money management. So, however you dedicate your time to earning money, it is important that your money is managed well and that you plan for your future.

Whatever educational path you decide to pursue after high school (college, trade school, military, certificate programs, etc.) will cost money . . . a lot of money. As you may already know, you have three options for paying for school:

- scholarships
- cash
- loans

One of the main purposes of this book is to have the necessary Conversations with you at a young enough age so that a scholarship is one of your realistic goals. Students with high GPAs, good test scores, a wealth of extra- and co-curricular activities, and internship and work experiences will get paid to go to school rather than pay for school. Colleges nearly fight one another for the top applicants.

This can and should be you.

You need to remember that while one college may not give you a scholarship, another might. Be smart in considering your options as you discuss them with your parents/mentors. Everybody has an opinion about student loans, so the best we can do is simply share our opinion, which is—they are worth it . . . to an extent. You must first exhaust several avenues before turning to loans. Those avenues are:

- scholarships
- family support
- working
- military service
- grants

If your family is not in a position to help you, you do not have enough scholarship money to cover all the costs (tuition, fees, living expenses, etc.), you aren't able to work enough hours to cover the costs, the military is not a good fit for you, or you don't qualify for grant money, then of course you should get a loan. Your education, if completed carefully, will no doubt allow you to get a good job and be able to pay back the loans, assuming you put in the work.

However, you need to decide what amount is worth paying for a college education. If you graduate with an overwhelming amount of debt, it may limit your opportunities later in life. Because of your student loan debt, you may be limited to looking at what a job pays you instead of how much you would enjoy it. Also, if you are thinking about going on after college and receiving an advanced degree, you may want to limit how much debt you go into for your undergraduate degree.

In the end, you need to consider several factors including, but not limited to:

- institutional fit
- prestige of the school
- location
- quality of the education
- cost of living

If you have worked hard enough to the point of getting into a prestigious university, then having a manageable loan would be worth the investment. You may feel underqualified right now, but the reason we are talking to you about this now is so you can be aware of your potential early enough to reach it.

Both of us have proven this theory in our own lives. We decided to take community college classes and later attend a public state university to complete our bachelor's degrees because, financially, it made sense.

However, the time came when we knew we had the potential, just like you, to think about and even attend prestigious academic programs. Now, you must know that if you are going for this type of goal because you want the recognition, then you have missed our point. The point is for you to be able to push yourself and be rewarded for your hard work. If you take middle school and high school seriously and come out with the credentials we've talked about, then you, too, will have more opportunities, and that is something you should never be ashamed to pursue!

One last thing we want to mention is the need for you to sacrifice at times. We have been inspired by examples around us. When other people had laptops, many of our friends used the library computers. When other people had their own cars, many used public transportation. When some friends were eating out, others chose to eat at the school cafeteria or go home for lunch.

These are the simple, daily sacrifices that will go a long way—not just for your wallet but also for the type of person you will become. When you're filling out the loan applications, the money may seem almost like Monopoly money—almost unreal because it just shows up after the loan application is done. Magic! Let us assure you that paying it back is far from magical.

LEARN. Blake shared a story about me, Bo, in Conversation 7, so I want to share a story with you about Blake and his family in this Conversation.

I have never met two people more dedicated to the envelope system than Blake and his wife, Staci. Staci in particular takes it to a whole new level.

I remember visiting their home once and seeing a color-coded, neatly labeled, accordion-style box of folders on their kitchen counter and asked Staci, "What is that?" She replied, "Our envelope system."

I was shocked. As we explained earlier, the envelope system is a technique used to manage your needs and wants. Blake and Staci literally withdraw the money they can spend for the month and use only that amount. It keeps them living below their means and forces them to save for the future.

Another reason I like using Blake and Staci as an example for this Conversation is that they have a total of four bachelor's degrees, a nursing degree, a master's degree, and a pending doctorate.

Crazy, right?

That's not even the coolest part. The four bachelor's degrees were all paid for by scholarship money, the nursing and master's degrees were 50 percent paid for through a scholarship and assistantship, respectively, and the pending doctorate is considerably discounted because Blake works for Purdue University.

Even though they received financial support while in school, Blake and Staci still maintained part-time jobs.

Together they have always researched every institution to make sure they would be happy and could afford the schooling. They are excellent examples of supporting their family together.

As you can tell, Blake and Staci LOVE education and have worked hard for it.

REFLECT. Please take as much time as you need to ponder the following questions. Then, with the help of your parents/mentors, fill in your responses in the space provided.

STUDENT ACCOUNTABILITY MODEL

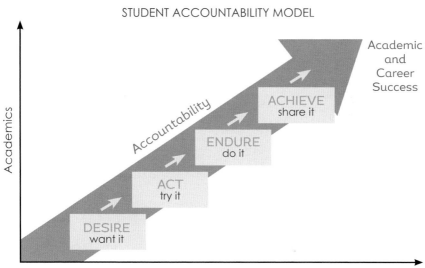

Application of 12 Conversations

How important is money to you? What type of lifestyle do you envision being happy with one day, and how much will it cost?

_____

_____

_____

_____

_____

_____

_____

What type of budgeting system can you set up today?

_____

_____

_____

_____

_____

_____

_____

_____

As you earn more money, how will your budgeting change?

_____

_____

_____

_____

_____

_____

_____

_____

Who do you look up to in terms of financial success? What can you learn about money management from that person's example?

_____

_____

_____

_____

_____

_____

_____

EXAMPLE

This page can be referenced as an example when filling out your own Money Management & Scholarships Action Sheet on the following page, or by downloading the template at http://www.theleaderinme.org/middleschoolsuccess.

PERSONAL MONTHLY INCOME STATEMENT

Income	
AMOUNT	DESCRIPTION
$40.00	Allowance
$10.00	Tennis lesson
$5.00	Spare change
$60.00	Presents
TOTAL: $115.00	

Expenses	
AMOUNT	DESCRIPTION
$2.25	Snack
$8.00	Movie
$5.25	Fast food
$35.96	New music
$63.54	Savings
TOTAL: $115.00	

MONEY MANAGEMENT & SCHOLARSHIPS

ACT. Routinely tracking the money you earn (income) and the money you spend (expenses) will allow you to better evaluate your current and future financial situation. Developing the habit of managing your finances is possible at your age and will provide you financial benefits in years to come. Please visit http://www .theleaderinme.org/middleschoolsuccess to download this template.

PERSONAL MONTHLY INCOME STATEMENT

Income	
AMOUNT	DESCRIPTION
TOTAL:	

Expenses	
AMOUNT	DESCRIPTION
TOTAL:	

A THOUGHT
TO PONDER

"If you dare nothing, then when the day is over, nothing is
all you will have gained."

—NEIL GAIMAN
ENGLISH AUTHOR OF SHORT FICTION, NOVELS, COMIC
BOOKS, GRAPHIC NOVELS, AUDIO THEATER, AND FILMS

CONVERSATION 10

COLLEGE APPLICATION PROCESS

LISTEN. Applying for anything can be an intimidating process, but you can follow certain principles no matter what you apply for. For the purposes of this book and Conversation, we will use the example of applying for admission to a college or university.

Does the college application process seem scary?

Don't worry. We can help you.

You need to be focused on two things:

- Be aware of deadlines.
- Be honest in the application process.

First things first: you can start early. Heck, you can start the process in middle school! Start writing down your extracurricular activities and internal work/service hours in middle school so you don't forget these experiences when it comes time to apply for college. Why not invite your family/friends and start going on campus tours of the colleges and universities near you? Once you cover those, then you can set goals to visit other schools of interest inside and outside of your state. How else will you know if they are a good fit for you? While you are touring different schools, think about what would make a good "institutional fit" for you. We are not making this up. A report was compiled by Gallup and Purdue University on this very issue. Their findings concluded that a student will be successful and happy when that student finds the following at an educational institution:

- purpose
- social well-being
- financial well-being
- community
- physical well-being

If you show up in person and get to know the people in the programs you are interested in, the advantage will be yours when the time comes to apply. It is much more valuable than just submitting an application online. Putting a name with a face and making a first impression is very powerful and, when done correctly, gives you an advantage.

A great phrase to keep in mind is "It never hurts to apply." You may be amazed by your options!

Through your campus visits you will be able to narrow down your options, a great benefit of starting early. When the time comes for actually applying in your senior year of high school, you will know where to apply. In terms of submitting your application, you must be aware of the various deadlines a college has. There will be some for "early" applications, "priority" applications, "regular" applications, and "late" applications, to name a few. These deadlines don't even include applying for federal financial aid, and they may or may not include scholarships.

The point is, know your deadlines!

One of the biggest mistakes high-school seniors make is thinking they have the whole year to apply to college. Most colleges offer their admissions application at the beginning of your senior year, and their scholarship deadlines keep moving up earlier and earlier, some even as early as November of the year before you graduate from high school. Now that you know this, do your research and plan accordingly.

While you are narrowing down your choices, take time to speak with your parents/mentors. There are fees involved in applying for each college, and you will want to make sure that you agree on how many colleges are an option. You can always be realistic about your budget, but be excited and hopeful about your options.

A great phrase to keep in mind is "It never hurts to apply." You may be amazed by your options!

In most cases, the same information will be required, and even the essays (if required) are similar. Keep an electronic copy of your essay(s) so they can be tweaked and adjusted for multiple applications so you don't have to start from scratch each time. The extra time and application fees that you spend may be worth it to have a few more options. Applications do not require any sort of commitment, so allow yourself the opportunity to choose from a good pool of schools.

Now that you understand the timing and expectations of the application process, we need to talk about the content of your application. Another key phrase to remember is "Honesty is the best policy."

While it is an old cliché, honesty truly is the best policy when filling out applications. Admissions selection committees are pretty good at knowing if you truly are who you say you are. They also rely on references and letters of recommendation in many cases. Plus, you want to be true to yourself and be proud of what you have rightfully and honestly accomplished. Even if you sneak past by lying, would you really want to get into a school or get a scholarship based on a lie?

Our whole point in having this Conversation with you now, at an early age, is to prepare you to know what selection committees look for and to encourage you to honestly strive for those qualities.

They look for:

- good grades
- solid test scores
- extra- and co-curricular involvement
- service

They also look for someone with goals who knows what it means to lead others—all of which we have discussed in this book. So be honest in your application and show what you've done to stand out.

If you do all of these things, you will certainly be unique because the majority of students applying do not have all of these points to boast about.

Also, you may have diverse experiences based on the way you were raised or because of traits you were born with. Tell them about those experiences. You have nothing to lose when you are honest with yourself and on your application.

Last, it never hurts to get to know people and ask for recommendations from those you already know. Every now and then you'll associate with the kind person who was paying attention and offers to write a letter or make a call on your behalf without being asked. Although that is the best-case scenario, it's not always realistic, and you should ask your mentors and other key people (teachers, supervisors, etc.) to become advocates on your behalf.

This is part of networking. Networking is a word many people use to describe the process of meeting people. The process could be as simple as getting someone's contact information or as deep as maintaining a lifelong friendship. For us, networking is about building relationships. Certainly, some relationships will be deeper than others; nevertheless, a relationship is more valuable than a one-time contact.

In the application process your networking will be beneficial. A letter of recommendation from a teacher who has known you for three years is a good example of a deep relationship. While not as deep, another example of good networking and building a relationship is contacting and meeting the admissions staff of the institution you would like to attend after high school.

This contact can be built into a relationship through:

- e-mails about your interest
- a personal visit to campus
- requests for advice about applying, housing, tuition costs, etc.

Be sure to start building this relationship before your senior year of high school!

LEARN. Jasmine is a friend of ours who received great direction from her mentors regarding the college application process. She lived in Pennsylvania and started the college-search process in eighth grade. It first started out as fun trips with her parents to nearby community colleges and universities. Her desire grew to learn more about other schools, and whenever Jasmine's family would travel to another state, they would stop at well-known universities for a tour or at least to walk around for a while. Her family also loved football, so Jasmine would study teams who came to play in her town and would find out more about their schools.

When it came time to apply for college, Jasmine applied to fifteen different institutions. The whole process of applying took about a month, but she ended up with seven offers to well-known universities. Her application highlighted her passion for, and involvement in, education. She was in several teaching societies and clubs and worked as a student teacher and volunteer in the local elementary school. Her GPA was high, and combined with her test scores, she did not have to come up with the funds to pay for tuition because of a scholarship. For the scholarship application, Jasmine was able to request letters of recommendation on her behalf from several teachers with whom she worked closely and who were able to write about her skills and potential. When she was ready to submit everything, she did so in person and was remembered from her campus tour and e-mail communications. Jasmine is a great example of how to manage the application process for college admissions and scholarships.

REFLECT. Please take as much time as you need to ponder the following questions. Then, with the help of your parents/mentors, fill in your answers in the space provided.

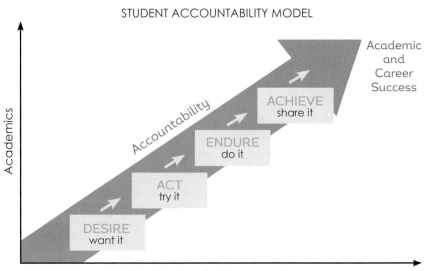

STUDENT ACCOUNTABILITY MODEL

What type of school would you like to attend after high school?

_____

_____

_____

What type of research would you need to start doing now for your future college-search process?

_____

_____

_____

_____

_____

What are typical admissions and scholarship deadlines for schools near you? What are typical application fees?

_____

_____

_____

_____

_____

How many schools could you realistically apply to for college, and which ones would they be? With your parents/mentors, make a list of them in order of your favorites.

_____

_____

_____

_____

_____

COLLEGE APPLICATION PROCESS

EXAMPLE

This page can be referenced as an example when filling out your own College Application Process Action Sheet on the following page, or by downloading the template at http://www .theleaderinme.org/middleschoolsuccess. This information is to be used as an example only. Please verify all information for yourself.

COLLEGE APPLICATION PREPARATION SHEET

Institution	Location	Deadlines for Admissions & Scholarships	General Admissions Require- ments	Contact Informa- tion	Costs
University of Nevada Las Vegas unlv.edu	Las Vegas, Nevada	Admissions July 1st Scholarships February 1st	Need a 3.0 minimum weighted GPA. Need a 22 or higher on ACT.	(xxx) xxx-xxxx	$60 application fee. $7,147 full-time, non-resident tuition and fees.
Dixie State University dixie.edu	St. George, Utah	Admissions August 1st Scholarships March 1st	No minimum GPA or test scores required. Students average 3.2 GPA and 20 on ACT.	(xxx) xxx-xxxx	$35 application fee. $2,145 full-time resident tuition and fees.
Stanford University stanford.edu	Stanford, California	Admissions January 2nd Scholarships January 2nd	75% of admitted students have a 4.0 GPA. 87% of admitted students have between a 30 and 36 on the ACT.	(xxx) xxx-xxxx	$90 application fee. $14,373 full-time, non-resident tuition and fees.
University of California Los Angeles ucla.edu	Los Angeles, California	Admissions November 30th Scholarships May 1st	Average 3.93 weighted GPA. Average ACT score of 29.	(xxx) xxx-xxxx	$70 application fee. $2,962 full-time, non-resident tuition and fees.
Southern Utah University suu.edu	Cedar City, Utah	Admissions April 1st Scholarships December 1st	Must have an index score of 90+ (see site for details).	(xxx) xxx-xxxx	$50 application fee. $2,962 full-time resident tuition and fees.

COLLEGE APPLICATION PROCESS

ACT. Take time to document your findings as you start to research the various colleges, universities, and other educational institutions that interest you. Collecting this information will help you narrow down your options based on what is most important to you, such as location, cost of attendance, and scholarship opportunities. Please visit http://www.theleaderinme.org /middleschoolsuccess to download this template.

COLLEGE APPLICATION PREPARATION SHEET

Institution	Location	Deadlines for Admissions & Scholarships	General Admissions Requirements	Contact Information	Costs

A THOUGHT
TO PONDER

"Fortune favors the prepared mind."

—DR. LOUIS PASTEUR
FRENCH CHEMIST AND MICROBIOLOGIST RENOWNED FOR
HIS DISCOVERIES OF THE PRINCIPLES OF VACCINATION,
MICROBIAL FERMENTATION, AND PASTEURIZATION

CONVERSATION 11

INTERVIEWING

LISTEN. Whether for an internship, for a scholarship, or for a job, interviews are intimidating but necessary. Interviewing is developmental—you get better with practice.

There are a couple of types of interviews. The typical interview we all think of is a high-stress situation where interviewees are trying to convince a person or a group of people that they are ready and qualified for whatever is at stake, such as a job. For this type of interview, we offer some basic tips:

> **TIP 1: Research the organization thoroughly beforehand.** Take the time to look at their website. What does it discuss? What do they do? Whom do they serve?

> **TIP 2: Dress appropriately and be professional.** Even if the company has a casual dress policy, it's always better to dress more professionally than you think you need to.

TIP 3: Be sure to come prepared. Bring a notepad and pen/pencil to take down any important information that may come up in conversation. This shows you are interested and prepared.

TIP 4: Be confident and enjoyable to be around. Smile! Organizations want to hire people who are confident, kind, and happy and whom they can visualize working well with.

TIP 5: Address by name the person(s) interviewing you. Chances are, you'll need to know it before the interview even begins because a receptionist will ask you whom you are meeting with! So learn the name early. And, if the interview was set up on the phone, ask if anyone else will be sitting in on the interview. That way you'll be more prepared.

TIP 6: Avoid lengthy responses to questions. Be short and to the point—practice out loud. But not too short! Answer the question as best as you can without rambling.

TIP 7: Beforehand, **think about and select some accomplishments and experiences** you can discuss if you are asked.

TIP 8: The end of every interview usually ends with the question: "Do you have any questions for us?" **Have one or two prepared.** Otherwise, you will appear uninterested in them and their company.

TIP 9: Recognize others by properly thanking those who helped with the interview process—parents/ mentors, administrative assistants, interviewers, etc. You may want to send a thank-you card to the person who interviewed you. Cards are a little pre-Internet, but they are still greatly appreciated.

These tips do not cover everything you will need to know to interview well. Other people have written entire books about this topic; nevertheless, we felt it necessary that you understand the basics at a young age. Keep in mind there are professionals at your school and in the community who can prepare you for an interview.

A word of caution: When you receive many opinions about presenting yourself in an interview, you may get overwhelmed and lose the sense of who you are. At some point you need to decide which advice is best for you personally and how to act accordingly because you will be more comfortable if you speak from your heart. You will smile more and be more comfortable if you come across as natural and welcoming. Be yourself and be honest in your answers. If you need more time to think about your answer, then ask your interviewer for a moment to think. A delayed, well-thought-out answer is much better than saying the first thing that comes to mind. Also, if you are asked about a skill you don't have, be honest, but indicate you are willing to do what it takes to acquire the skill.

Another type of interview is one where you seek out a specific individual with whom you would like to meet and either learn about the work he or she does and/or ask for potential job or internship opportunities. For example, if you want to work at a law firm one day, understanding what a lawyer does and connecting with one at a local firm is important. You can do this by going to a website, asking around, or directly calling a company. This process can be intimidating, but almost every professional we know is willing to help young students.

As you go through this process, introduce yourself properly to the

Be confident and enjoyable to be around.

Smile!

Organizations want to hire people who are confident, kind, and happy and whom they can visualize working well with.

professional, and express your desire to learn. Do not ask for more than a simple twenty-minute conversation, and wait to see where it goes from there. Be sure to express gratitude for the time spent with you.

These types of interviews are called informational interviews. We recommend doing them frequently. They can be with business owners, alumni of a college you're interested in attending, family members, neighbors, etc. Most people are flattered when you want to talk to them about their accomplishments and learn from their experiences. It makes them feel valued because you sincerely respect the work they do.

Remember, interviewing is a skill. As you interview, you will get better. Start practicing now by increasing the amount of face-to-face time you spend with those around you. Technology is crushing this important life skill, and we worry about you, our young friend, being able to become an effective interpersonal communicator. We know you can use technology to better our world, but please do not forget the value of looking someone in the eye and having a meaningful conversation.

LEARN. We want to tell you about Louis, a person Blake interviewed one time for a scholarship. When Louis came to his interview, he was not a new face. He had interacted with several other students online and showed a genuine interest in the program.

This interaction established a solid first impression. Additionally, when Blake received Louis's résumé, he could tell it was detailed and well written.

Louis walked into the interview with a smile on his face, dressed in a suit, and introduced himself. As Louis sat down, he didn't appear to be nervous. He was engaged in the interview, and Blake could see this because of the way he sat and the way he listened intently to the questions.

He was prepared for each question and gave brief, direct responses, highlighting his experiences and abilities with confidence. Louis was not afraid to show his sense of humor and was comfortable, yet maintained a professional image.

When asked a particularly difficult question, Louis asked Blake if he could take a second to think about his response. He then took out a folder, flipped through some notes, and gave a well-thought-out answer. When Blake asked Louis if he had any questions, he revealed his research about the scholarship and asked the questions he had prepared. After Louis's interview, it was clear he was the right candidate for the scholarship.

REFLECT. Please take as much time as you need to ponder the following questions. Then, with the help of your parents/mentors, fill in your answers in the space provided.

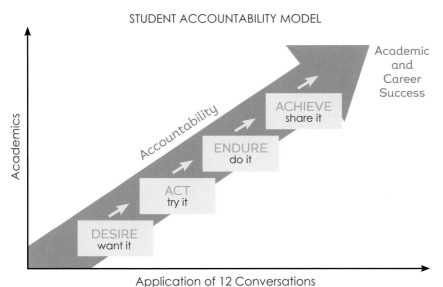

STUDENT ACCOUNTABILITY MODEL

Academic and Career Success

Academics

Accountability

ACHIEVE
share it

ENDURE
do it

ACT
try it

DESIRE
want it

Application of 12 Conversations

Who would you like to have informational interviews with?

_____

_____

_____

_____

_____

_____

What interviewing resources are available to you?

_____

_____

_____

_____

_____

_____

When and with whom can you practice for a job interview?

_____

_____

_____

_____

_____

_____

How can your parents/mentors help you practice for interviews?

_____

_____

_____

_____

_____

_____

_____

INTERVIEWING

EXAMPLE

This page can be referenced as an example when filling out your own Interviewing Action Sheet on the following page, or by downloading the template at http://www.theleaderinme.org /middleschoolsuccess.

INTERVIEW PREPARATION	
Job description	• Intern — Riverton Community Theater • Hiring a part-time intern to help with summer productions of "Wizard of Oz" and "The Pale Pink Dragon"
Names of interviewers	• Rosa Mueller, Director • David Odette, Stage Manager
Research	• Riverton Community Theater performed "Oliver" and "The Phantom of the Opera" last year. • Rosa Mueller has been the director for three years. • David Odette is new this year. • Most plays are sold out; however, attendance is decreasing and budgets are tight according to people I've talked to in past plays.
Requirements (basic and preferred)	• Basic — free time after school, available during most practices and all productions. • Preferred — background and interest in theater, music, and dance.
Matching strengths with requirements	• Basic — free in the summers and each production day; great planning skills. • Preferred — member of the drama club at school and taking piano lessons; also I am around many young people whom I could market to.
Weaknesses to address if asked	• I'm a little young and inexperienced, but I have the desire and potential to contribute for at least a few years.
Related experiences	• I've been in two school plays, one of which I was the lead role; I am in the drama club and take theater classes at school; talk about the time I had to sing without a microphone or the time I forgot my lines and improvised and nobody could tell.
Questions for committee	• What are the top three things an intern could do to be valuable? • How do they help their interns learn more about a career in acting?
People to thank	• Rosa - interviewer • David - interviewer • Mike - assistant

136

INTERVIEWING

ACT. As you begin to have informational and professional interviews, it is nice to be prepared beforehand. The sections below can be filled in prior to an interview. Use these notes to aid you in effectively answering interview questions. Be sure to thank your interviewers and anyone who helped you schedule the interview. Please visit http://www.theleaderinme.org/middleschoolsuccess to download this template.

INTERVIEW PREPARATION	
Job description	
Names of interviewers	
Research	
Requirements (basic and preferred)	
Matching strengths with requirements	
Weaknesses to address if asked	
Related experiences	
Questions for committee	
People to thank	

A THOUGHT
TO PONDER

———•⟨ ⟩•———

"We cannot teach people anything; we can only help them discover it within themselves."

—GALILEO GALILEI
ITALIAN ASTRONOMER, PHYSICIST, MATHEMATICIAN,
ENGINEER, AND PHILOSOPHER

CONVERSATION

12

SHARE YOUR EXPERIENCE

LISTEN. We have reached the last Conversation and, in our opinion, the most important. We have mentioned throughout this book that sharing your experience and continually giving back are necessary components of success. The eleven previous Conversations are designed to increase your desire to act upon factors that contribute to academic success, as seen in the Student Accountability Model.

Nothing you read in this book will be of any benefit to you unless you apply it to your own life. Just as you've heard probably your whole life: It will go in one ear and out the other. If you want to live it, you have to share it.

How do you do that? You teach it.

Dr. Stephen R. Covey referred to it as "Three-Person Teaching."
He said:

> One of the most important things you can do is to share these ideas with others: with your family, with your friends, and associates. Don't just retell what you've learned, but talk about the insights you've acquired and the ideas you want to implement. Because that's where the real learning takes place. It is in the teaching and in the sharing. . . . Share insights into what has worked for you and what has not. . . . Set goals to improve in specific areas. . . . Revisit the commitments you've made to yourself.

Once you feel that you have reached a level of success in a particular Conversation, share what you have learned and help others around you—maybe a classmate or a younger sibling.

We know you will be presented with many opportunities to help others achieve their potential. Do not overlook these opportunities. Small and large acts of kindness and taking the time to mentor others can go a long way.

Let's talk about those who helped you get to where you are! Achieving academic success requires the help of others, and it is important that you recognize when you are being helped.

Say thank you! Write a handwritten thank-you note. Never underestimate its power! It sounds like such a simple act, and it is. But it means a lot to those who receive it.

For example, let's say you received help from your aunt in preparing a science fair project. We are pretty sure she wouldn't charge you for her time because she loves you and wants to help you. This is perfect because, as a student, you don't have the money to pay for this help; however, a handwritten thank-you note is all you need. She will feel valued and appreciate your kindness.

When writing thank-you notes, be specific and thoughtful. Mail the note or take it to the recipient in a timely manner. People don't expect this type of recognition, so it makes the gesture very rewarding.

We know you're busy, so we'll provide you with a little tip. Have some thank-you cards and stamps ready for such opportunities. Keep them ready in a drawer. Otherwise, you'll forget. Trust us. We know.

Another form of giving back when someone helps you is recognizing his or her efforts with some sort of gift. Be thoughtful with the gift by paying attention to clues. For example, if your teacher writes you a letter of recommendation and you happen to know he loves fishing, then maybe a fishing-themed gift would be appropriate to express your gratitude. Give simple, thoughtful gifts that are not out of your price range. Gifts are not something people expect, so anything you give is a surprise.

You can also publicly acknowledge those who have helped you. We feel pretty confident that you have strong social-media skills. Use those! Express your appreciation on Facebook, Twitter, Instagram, or any other accounts we are too old to know about.

Nothing you read in this book will be of any benefit to you unless you personalize it to your own life.

Just as you've heard probably your whole life: It will go in one ear and out the other.

If you want to live it, you have to share it.

How do you do that?

You teach it.

Finally, just spending time with someone and listening is a powerful way of giving back. Follow the same steps in each Conversation of this book—listen, learn, reflect, and act. Giving back is also about sharing what you feel and have learned through certain experiences. The ultimate academic success is not the fact that you personally achieved it. The ultimate academic success is reached when you inspire and help another person achieve his or her potential, and this is done most effectively as you reflect upon your own journey to academic success.

LEARN. This is the only Conversation where we are not going to provide you an example of someone who shared his or her experience and gave back. We would like to try a little experiment. Who gave you this book? Be honest . . . we know you most likely didn't rush out to buy it yourself. Write a thank-you note to this person and see what happens to your relationship. You will not regret it. Instead of our giving you a story to read, you are writing your own.

REFLECT. Please take as much time as you need to ponder the following questions. Then, with the help of your parents/mentors, fill in your responses in the space provided.

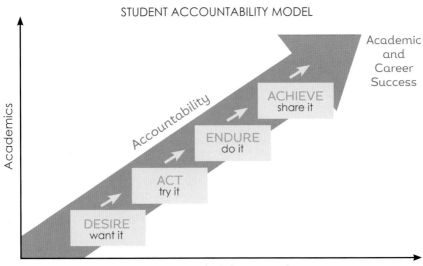

STUDENT ACCOUNTABILITY MODEL

Academic and Career Success

ACHIEVE
share it

ENDURE
do it

ACT
try it

DESIRE
want it

Accountability

Academics

Application of 12 Conversations

How do you personally see yourself recognizing someone else?

_____

_____

_____

_____

_____

Who are you currently not recognizing that you should be?

_____

_____

_____

_____

_____

Who will you teach this content to? What do you want to share with that person?

_____

_____

_____

_____

_____

Discuss with your parents/mentors what academic success means to you.

_____

_____

_____

_____

_____

SHARE YOUR EXPERIENCE

EXAMPLE

This page can be referenced as an example when filling out your own Share Your Experience Action Sheet on the following page, or by downloading the template at http://www.theleaderinme.org /middleschoolsuccess.

SHARE YOUR EXPERIENCE

Name	Title	Contact Info	Action	Notes
Rosa Mueller	Director, Riverton Community Theater	123 Thespian Way, Riverton, PA 84065	Thank-you note for interview	Rosa wanted an intern to be passionate about a career in theater.
Sam	Best friend	Next-door neighbor	Helped him with math homework	Get him a calculator.
Ms. Kinzer	Advisor, National Honor Society	RHS Room 141, 12300 S. 2700 W., Riverton, PA 84065	Thank-you gift for writing me a letter of recommendation	She loves lapel pins.
Mom	Mom	My house	Birthday card	Her birthday is Friday.

SHARE YOUR EXPERIENCE

ACT. Always strive to recognize the efforts of those who assist you in your journey to academic success and look for personal opportunities to help others. Keep detailed notes of ways to express your gratitude for those who support you (write a note, send a gift, make a phone call, visit together, etc.) and act upon your ideas. In addition, dedicate time to help mentor others (tutoring, advising, volunteering, serving, etc.). Please visit http://www.theleaderinme .org/middleschoolsuccess to download this template.

SHARE YOUR EXPERIENCE

Name	Title	Contact Info	Action	Notes

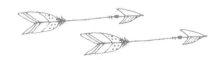

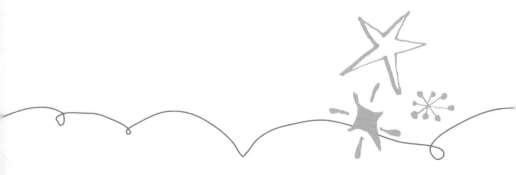

Concluding
THOUGHTS

Thank you for taking the time to read *The Middle School Student's Guide to Academic Success: 12 Conversations for College and Career Readiness*. As we've presented the 12 Conversations to other middle school students and parents/mentors, it has been rewarding to see their excitement. A light turns on that wasn't there before. We are confident you, too, are excited about academic success and have a desire to achieve it. We understand you may feel a bit overwhelmed; however, these feelings are natural and much better than the feelings you will have later if you do not prepare for higher education now. Don't give up!

In order to organize everything we've discussed throughout this book, we've created a Summary Guide that lists the main points you learned from each Conversation. Use your guide as a checklist of progress. We've also included an example for your reference.

Do not give up; keep trying. We know that you can do amazing things. And when—not if—you have, thank those who helped you along the way.

SUMMARY GUIDE

This page can be referenced as an example when filling out your own summary guide on the following page, or by downloading the template at http://www.theleaderinme.org/middleschoolsuccess.

01
Goals
- ❏ Always keep an updated list of your top six life goals.
- ❏ Make sure your goals are detailed.
- ❏ Utilize parents/mentors.

02
Planning & Preparation
- ❏ Set aside time to plan and prepare daily.
- ❏ Plan ahead—especially for the next six months.
- ❏ Don't forget to research, research, research . . . and then plan.

03
Time Management
- ❏ Utilize your preferred time-management tool.
- ❏ Keep an organized to-do list.
- ❏ Use reminders and write down important dates and deadlines.

04
Grade Point Average (GPA)
- ❏ Your GPA is based on hard work—always track it.
- ❏ Never, ever cheat.
- ❏ Take time when selecting classes and teachers.

05
Extra- & Co-Curricular Activities
- ❏ Get involved in both extra- and co-curricular activities.
- ❏ The more diverse you are, the better—do what is fun and relevant to your goals.
- ❏ Avoid wasting time—don't be lazy—be actively engaged.

06
Service
- ❏ Never underestimate the value of volunteering and serving others.
- ❏ Consider starting a club or group that you're passionate about.
- ❏ Find ways to build your leadership experience through service.

07
College Entrance Exams
- ❏ Don't wait to take the exam without practicing.
- ❏ Don't get frustrated with low scores; keep trying as long as it takes.
- ❏ Take the ACT/SAT at least three times before your senior year of high school.

08
Internships & Work Experience
- ❏ Start thinking about what career and lifestyle you desire.
- ❏ Build a résumé and constantly update it.
- ❏ Represent yourself professionally both in person and online.

09
Money Management & Scholarships
- ❏ Create and continually use a personal income statement.
- ❏ Do not spend more than you make and start the habit of saving money regularly.
- ❏ Research scholarship opportunities at schools and other organizations.

10
College Application Process
- ❏ Identify the top five institutions you could see yourself attending after high school.
- ❏ Understand the application process and deadlines at the institutions you want to attend.
- ❏ It is very beneficial to visit campuses and meet people in person before applying.

11
Interviewing
- ❏ Frequently seek out opportunities to conduct informational interviews.
- ❏ Utilize the professional career services and interviewing resources around you.
- ❏ Be prepared (research, professionalism, practice, memorized experiences, etc.).

12
Share Your Experience
- ❏ True success is not just personal achievement but also occurs when you help others achieve their potential.
- ❏ Notes and small gifts are good ways to recognize others.
- ❏ You will personally benefit the more you give back and recognize others.

SUMMARY GUIDE

Now is the time for you to write the main points you have learned from each Conversation. Please visit http://www.theleaderinme.org/middleschoolsuccess to download this template.

01
Goals

- ❏
- ❏
- ❏

02
Planning & Preparation

- ❏
- ❏
- ❏

03
Time Management

- ❏
- ❏
- ❏

04
Grade Point Average (GPA)

- ❏
- ❏
- ❏

05
Extra- & Co-Curricular Activities

- ❏
- ❏
- ❏

06
Service

- ❏
- ❏
- ❏

07
College Entrance Exams

- ❏
- ❏
- ❏

08
Internships & Work Experience

- ❏
- ❏
- ❏

09
Money Management & Scholarships

- ❏
- ❏
- ❏

10
College Application Process

- ❏
- ❏
- ❏

11
Interviewing

- ❏
- ❏
- ❏

12
Share Your Experience

- ❏
- ❏
- ❏

ABOUT THE AUTHORS

Blake and Bo Nemelka grew up in Utah, where they graduated from South Hills Middle School and Riverton High School. They continued their education together at Utah State University, where they were selected to be student ambassadors and played for the university tennis team. The brothers each took a hiatus in their education to provide humanitarian service. Blake volunteered in Lima, Peru, and Bo volunteered in Merida, Mexico.

Upon their return, Blake and Bo continued their education at Utah State University. They were both selected as Huntsman Scholars and graduated with honors from the Jon M. Huntsman School of Business. Blake later attended Vanderbilt University, where he graduated with his master's degree in education administration, and Bo attended Yale University, where he graduated with his master's degree in health-care management. Blake and Bo are each happily married with young children, and continue their love for education in their personal and professional lives.

Does Your School Empower Every Student to Be a Leader?

LEAD is a schoolwide model that equips middle-school students with the leadership and life skills necessary to succeed in the twenty-first century. *LEAD* Schools seamlessly integrate the 7 Habits and other leadership development into daily curriculum, activities, and culture. Through this approach, schools create a culture of student empowerment where students learn to set and achieve meaningful goals, take responsibility for their learning, work well with others, and use their individual talents to better the school community.

"We only get one chance to prepare our students for a future none of us can possibly predict. What are we going to do with that one chance?"

- Muriel Summers

Learn more at www.TheLeaderinMe.org or call 1-800-272-6839

FranklinCovey | EDUCATION